To Lina
Best Wis
from
Gill

GILLIAN GRIFFITH

Fergus and Lavinia

One Man's Egg Is A Woman's Frittata

Mereo Books

2nd Floor, 6-8 Dyer Street, Cirencester, Gloucestershire, GL7 2PF
An imprint of Memoirs Books. www.mereobooks.com
and www.memoirsbooks.co.uk

Title of Book: Fergus and Lavinia
ISBN: 978-1-86151-973-3

First published in Great Britain in 2020
by Mereo Books, an imprint of Memoirs Books.

Copyright ©2020

Gillian Griffith has asserted her right under the Copyright Designs and Patents
Act 1988 to be identified as the author of this work.

A CIP catalogue record for this book is available from the British Library.
This book is sold subject to the condition that it shall not by way of trade
or otherwise be lent, resold, hired out or otherwise circulated without the
publisher's prior consent in any form of binding or cover, other than that in
which it is published and without a similar condition, including this condition
being imposed on the subsequent purchaser.

The address for Memoirs Books can be
found at www.mereobooks.com

Mereo Books Ltd. Reg. No. 12157152

Typeset in 11/15pt Century Schoolbook
by Wiltshire Associates.
Printed and bound in Great Britain

For Jo, Maggie, Alison and 'Writers On The Edge'.

Contents

Introduction

1. Differences 1
2. The Trouble with Grass 5
3. Points of View 11
4. The F in Food, Fergus and InFuriating 18
5. Fergus Does Some Shopping 25
6. Storm in a Quick Wash 34
7. Fergus Finds His Muse 41
8. Lavinia Embarks on a Creative Journey 51
9. Just Another Thursday 60
10. A Weekend Break 68
11. A Question of Pockets 77
12. Out of the Comfort Zone 85
13. Enter Charlie, Stage Left 95
14. Old Peculier 102
15. No Cause for Alarm 114
16. One False Move 122
17. Drama in W H Smith's 128
18. Festive Spirit 140

Introduction

Fergus and Lavinia are figments of the author's imagination, born out of idle musing on the forces that govern social interactions. Not a common subject in the casual musing category, you might think. So let me quickly add that my interest is not, in any sense, academic. I am simply an observer of the human condition and, in particular, of the relationships we humans make, break, endure or have thrust upon us.

My current status as a fully paid-up member of the long-term relationship fraternity led me to the idea that I was perfectly placed to focus a lens on such a couple. This is not to suggest that Fergus and Lavinia are in any way typical; far from it. But they were amenable to my proposal to explore both the commonplace and the bizarre aspects of rubbing along together for the duration. Obviously there are serious issues associated with advancing years. In these stories I have chosen to leave those things hovering on the periphery. I've taken instead a light-hearted look at the idiosyncrasies, niggles and grumbles that sometimes become integral features in long-term relationships.

In truth, or in this case fiction, Fergus and Lavinia have much in common with Jack Spratt and his wife, so you may wonder what attracted them to each other in the first instance. The answer lies in a form of verbal fisticuffs. Their paths first crossed in a university debating society, where they were frequently on opposing sides. Fergus, despite a ruthless desire to defeat his opponents, secretly admired Lavinia's ability to slice through an argument and expose its flaws. Although exasperated by Fergus' trick of distracting her with hyperbole, she was nevertheless intrigued by his encyclopaedic knowledge. Outside the debating forum Fergus, passionate Art student and Lavinia, reading English Literature, found they had much in common and also plenty to argue about. Neither of them would admit to having fallen in love, but they became comfortably wrapped up in each other. So comfortable, in fact, that it took Lavinia considerably longer than she had anticipated to manoeuvre Fergus into a position where he thought it might be a good idea to ask her to marry him. Had he been aware of Lavinia's plans to 'sort him out', he might have had second thoughts.

We catch up with the pair almost half a century later as they begin to settle into their retirement. They have become established members of their rural village community, although it would be fair to say Lavinia is more integrated than Fergus. Their relationship is still sound, but some of the edges are roughened and patience is occasionally in short supply. The dynamics of their union unfold in a series of random snapshots of events in the lives of Fergus the impossible and Lavinia the indomitable.

CHAPTER 1

Differences

Fergus has always known that when it comes to food, he and Lavinia are in different leagues. Fergus' shepherd's pie is Lavinia's lasagne and her spaghetti Bolognese is his meatballs in gravy. Marriage, thus far, has been a journey of compromises, mostly on Lavinia's part, as Fergus is not easily persuaded away from his comfort zone. The cake forks are a case in point, and they were the first things to be returned to their leather box.

'It's cake. I've got fingers Lavinia. Why complicate it?'

Next to go was the butter knife, on account of the butter becoming contaminated by chutney or strawberry jam and occasionally both if Fergus had been home alone. He did eventually concede that a napkin could be useful, although, every now and then, one found its way into his pocket and embarked on a new life as a paint rag in his studio.

Lavinia is partial to a hearty venison casserole. Fergus favours a good rabbit stew, to which she turns up her nose and pronounces, 'Peasant cooking, like egg and chips.'

'Nothing wrong with that. It's good tasty stuff.'

'Oh, I know it's decent food, but you wouldn't want it every day, would you?'

'I don't see why not, but then I couldn't eat your lamb and pomegranate thing every day either. It's a question of chalk and cheese I guess.'

Their differences had not been quite so pronounced when they started out together. Student paupers both, they had scoured the markets in the sixties for cheap fruit and veg and the butcher's special offers. Lunch was frequently a mug of hot soup with a chunk of yesterday's bread. Tea was often fried egg sandwiches and Sunday dinner a glorious pan of corned beef hash. Lavinia had found it very hard. She'd broken out sometimes and taken herself off to the café in Marshall and Colgrove for a pot of Earl Grey and an iced bun, just to remind herself of how the other half lived.

When Fergus had a few spare pennies, he made straight for the Polish corner shop. He bought seeded bread, salted butter and a jar of apricot conserve which Lavinia willingly shared after observing that, for the same money, they could have had Polish potato pancakes or four slices of *makowiec*, poppy seed cake with almonds and honey. Fergus considered poppy seeds to be food for birds. He still does.

Fergus has, however, learned over the years to tolerate and sometimes even enjoy oregano and basil, tarragon and dill, as long as they are subtle. He can do parsley but not in white sauce, and he has become quite partial to a dab of *Dijon* on his steak or a hint of horseradish with his mackerel. But even now he can't make first base with coriander, chilli or curry and, after what he described as a near-death experience with shellfish, he only has to look at a prawn to put his stomach on emergency alert.

Lavinia gets more than a little exasperated with him at times and Fergus understands why, but it seems to him that pragmatism is the order of the day as they drift into their dotage.

'You have whatever you like, old thing. I'm quite happy with an egg,' he tells her.

Lavinia finds that difficult to deal with. But in his youth Fergus had been a committed vegetarian and had survived on eggs because, in those days, no mother of seven had time to faff about 'food for one'. It was a strange thing but, for Fergus, chips and egg still hit the spot after all this time.

He and Lavinia are slowly evolving into Jack Spratt and his wife, he who would eat no fat and she who would eat no lean. Fergus eats shredded wheat. Lavinia has yoghurt with berries. He has a wholemeal cheese sandwich. She has smoked salmon and cream cheese on rye. They occasionally enjoy a roast chicken or a leg of lamb together and so far, they haven't fallen out over vegetables. However, Fergus is really struggling with Lavinia's current passion for aubergine, sweet potato and butternut squash, and it's rapidly reaching the point where he is going to have to tell her.

CHAPTER 2

The Trouble with Grass

The day the lawn tractor died was a defining moment in the lives of Fergus and Lavinia. For the last fifteen years, between March and November, Fergus and the tractor had grumbled around the paddock every Saturday morning with increasingly bad grace. Several times each season Fergus was heard to pronounce, mostly to Lavinia, 'I can't imagine what possessed us to buy a house with a field!'

Of course, in the early days, it had made an excellent football pitch, tennis court, racetrack, and general area for letting off steam if they had young visitors. Occasionally, if the tractor was outside, someone would ask Fergus if they could have a go and he would happily hand over the keys, along with instructions to start at the perimeter and drive in ever-decreasing loops towards the centre, thus saving him a job.

There was a point when Fergus indulged his artistic streak and drove the tractor in random fashion, creating islands of rough grass which he allowed to do their own thing, effectively reducing mowing time by fifty percent for one year. But as he had not thought it through properly, the following spring, the neglected herbage had become rampant and the lawn tractor said 'No!'

Lavinia kept a very low profile while Fergus hacked back his wild islands with a scythe.

'What you need on there is a pony or two,' smirked Henry, their horsey neighbour from up the lane, as he leaned over the gate to watch. 'I've got a couple as would sort that lot in no time for you.'

Fergus knew it irked Henry to see good grass going to waste. 'Forget it!' he said. 'I'm not swapping mowing for muck shovelling. If it were up to me the whole lot could go wild, but someone gets very uppity about weeds invading her garden.'

'Ah well, suit yourself,' Henry replied, disappearing back behind the hedge.

After the lawn tractor had finally expired, Lavinia was not entirely surprised when Fergus announced that he had no intention of replacing it. His paddock mowing days were over, which left Lavinia with a problem, because she was proud of her garden and she did like things neat and tidy. The unavoidable truth was that they were both feeling their age and the garden demanded too much of their time. Neither was as fit or as flexible as they once were, and whereas they used to spend whole days outside, lately it had shrunk to a couple of hours, a cup of tea and a tidy up. They had replaced the back-breaking herbaceous borders with rose beds and reduced the vegetable garden by half, still providing for their own needs and those of the freezer.

The issue of the paddock was not pressing as autumn was fast approaching, but nevertheless Lavinia felt the need for some kind of a plan since Fergus had obviously given up on it. She wandered outside to cut a bunch of fragrant yellow 'Poet's Wife' to give her inspiration. When she had arranged them to her satisfaction, she settled herself at the kitchen table with a fresh pot of coffee and a slice of Mary Berry's Lemon Drizzle. A pristine sheet of A3 paper purloined from Fergus' sketch pad was spread in front of her.

Using a black felt tip she wrote *Paddock Facts* in large letters and started a list.

Lawn tractor dead.
Grass grows.
Fergus opted out.

Reflecting on these while she ate her cake, she added:

Something has to be done!

She underlined all the facts with a red felt tip, which made a satisfying squeak on the top-quality cartridge paper. She poured herself another coffee and began a second list, headed *Possible Solutions*.

New machine? Unlikely but possible.
Pony? Non-starter.
Grass-eating creatures? Sheep? Goats? Probably more trouble than grass.

Think outside the box, she told herself, but the best she could conjure up was *Borrow creatures*. To which she swiftly added '*Not Cows!*' She couldn't tolerate cowpats or indiscriminate mooing at dawn.

Considering the potential donors of acceptable livestock, Lavinia reluctantly came to the unsettling conclusion that horses were the only possible contenders. She wrote HORSES on the page in small capitals.

Lavinia hated horses as much as Fergus hated grass. This was not where she had been hoping 'brainstorming' would lead. She felt quite disheartened, and in a sudden fit of pique she drew a large box half the width of the page and wrote inside it:

Withdraw savings. Buy new lawn tractor. Persuade Fergus to use it.

It was never going to happen. She knew that. Beneath the box she scrawled

Fat chance!

The whole exercise had been thoroughly depressing. Lavinia sighed deeply and reached into the cupboard for the biscuit tin. She picked out the last three chocolate cookies and ate them in quick succession.

When Fergus ambled into the kitchen, he found her staring gloomily at her scribblings.

'Any coffee going?'

She handed him the empty coffee pot and winced as he spattered coffee grounds all over her sparkling Belfast sink.

'Well, you'll be pleased to know I've sorted out the paddock. Any of those chocolate cookies left?'

Lavinia raised her eyebrows to his statement and then shook her head in answer to his question.

'Shortbread?' he tried hopefully, before selecting plain digestives and continuing to talk through the crumbs.

'Yes, it was quite fortuitous really. I bumped into old Scottie from the hunt kennels when I was down at the post box. I was telling him about the mower packing up and he mentioned he'd got a couple of quietish hunters he could put on the paddock for a week or two to take the grass right down for the winter. He's bringing them over in a day or two. I just have to check for weak spots in the fence at the far end of the garden. Wouldn't want clomping beasts trampling your precious roses, would we? Oh, don't look at me like that old thing. It'll be fine. Will you have another coffee? I've made enough for two.'

Biscuits in one hand and mug in the other, Fergus glanced down at the table on his way to the door.

'Starting a new project?'

'No, not really,' Lavinia replied, folding the paper in half and half again.

'Good to keep the grey cells on their toes though eh? Right then, I'll leave you to it and go and rattle that fence a bit. See what's what.'

Lavinia tore the sheet of paper into four, eight, sixteen, thirty-two and beyond until she'd made a small pile of high-quality confetti. She glanced at the clock. It was almost three minutes past twelve. Time enough, she thought and walked into the sitting room, where she poured herself an extra-large glass of sherry.

CHAPTER 3

Points of View

Lavinia

It is March the twenty-first. Just another day. Well, almost.

The date is etched into Lavinia's consciousness. Her thoughts hurtle backwards through the decades as she recalls the people who were present. A good proportion are long gone, and the rest have forgotten. She gave up reminding him years ago when she finally accepted that it was a fruitless exercise and decided that if it wasn't spontaneous then there really was little point. Instead, on this day every year she puts on her pearls and takes him out for lunch – her treat.

He raises his eyebrows when she tells him she'll have a

large glass of Shiraz and looks stunned when she orders a fillet steak. He sticks with shepherds' pie, which is always a safe option, but then he's never been one for pushing the boat out even when his own wallet is not involved.

He declines a dessert and sips half a pint of Bishop's Finger while Lavinia demolishes a huge piece of chocolate torte with extra cream.

'Is the pudding good?'

'Yes, it's delicious and very chocolatey.'

'Jolly well ought to be at that price.'

'You should have had something. They do apple pie.'

He shakes his head. 'Spoils the taste of the beer.'

Lavinia leans back in her seat and dabs her mouth with her napkin. She raises her glass.

'Here's to us then,' she says before draining it.

'Absolutely, old thing,' he replies.

Fergus

Fergus is standing by the kitchen window hugging his third mug of coffee and contemplating mowing the grass. It's already the twenty-first of March. He's done very well to put it off until now, but there are rain clouds, so he probably won't start today either.

'Can you believe it's nearly the end of March?' he says without turning round.

'Yes, of course I can. The daffodils have been out for ages. I was thinking we might go out for lunch today... my treat?'

'Well, I was planning to tackle the grass,' he says, 'but I guess it'll go another day. So okay, let's do that.'

He can't remember the last time they'd had lunch out, at her suggestion, but it must be about a year ago. Yes, just about a year.

He is aware that they don't do much gadding about together these days. She sees her friends and goes to one or two group things. He can't abide groups. He does meet his three close friends, individually and in strict rotation, for a beer and a bite to eat, but only on an *ad hoc* basis.

He observes that Lavinia has dressed up for lunch. That isn't his kind of thing. However, he has changed his pullover and run a comb through his hair.

While they wait for their meals to arrive, he tries to engage her in his plans for the veg patch, but she seems disinterested. He gives up, sips his half pint, and falls to wondering if he should move the wigwam for the runner beans or just fork in a load of compost. He watches the waitress out of the corner of his eye. She's a fine figure of a girl; strong black-stockinged thighs beneath a short skirt. She sees him looking and flashes him a bright red lipsticky smile that makes him feel every one of his three-score years and ten. He looks across at his wife. She is still a good-looking woman, but something is bugging her today and he is damned if he knows what it is.

Daisy Parker is sitting by the window stirring the froth into her cappuccino and wondering if the Rose and Crown was a bad idea after all. Her task for creative writing this week is to prepare an observational study of interaction between two real-life characters and use it as the foundation for a short story. The Rose and Crown is on the main road, a little way out of town and therefore, Daisy had reasoned, might have more potential for characters. Just my luck to pick a quiet day, she muses.

The lone drinkers at the bar are no use to her at all and Daisy swiftly dismisses the rowdy family with two teenagers and a toddler. Obviously a second marriage and, inevitably, too complicated for short fiction.

The young couple eating burgers and chips are together in body, but each lost in their separate worlds on their iPhones. Zero interaction there.

I'll finish my coffee and scoot, she thinks.

The elderly couple arrive as she gathers her things preparing to leave. They are an incongruous pair, for sure. I'll give them five minutes, she decides. The wife, for she could be nothing other, judging by her fixed expression and tightly buttoned body language, has clearly made an effort with her appearance. Daisy's initial appraisal notes the matching pearl necklace and earrings, the coordinated bag and shoes and the flashy jewelled ring. The husband, on the other hand, has obviously come in from the garden at the last minute, washed his hands and combed his hair but failed to consider his good quality but well-worn muddy shoes.

These two could be just what I'm looking for, thinks Daisy. She orders another coffee and takes out her notebook.

After several minutes she concludes there's not much chemistry between them, but the electricity around the wife almost crackles. He's clearly making an effort to chat, but she's not engaging at all. He gives up and turns his attention to the waitress instead. This prompts Daisy to speculate on why they've come out for lunch. There may be clues in their choice of food of course, but it is equally possible they are just a couple of old dears who come out once a week, for fish and chips on a plate, to save her cooking. Something tells Daisy that is not the case. She sips her coffee and doodles her ideas on her pad.

She is too far away to see what they have ordered, but the wife has an oval platter with lots of trimmings so, at a guess, it's probably a steak. His meal arrives in a dish with an accompanying bowl of mixed vegetables which he tips out onto a plate along with the content of the dish. It looks like shepherds' pie. Daisy's interest is rekindled.

Two possible themes present themselves. Either he is

treating her or, and this one carries more weight, she is treating herself.

He is not behaving like a man spoiling his lady wife. She seems to be making some kind of statement, but he's certainly not getting it. Daisy goes back to her ideas and doodles, trying to imagine what he might have done to annoy her, but none of her theories would be likely to culminate in a mid-week lunch out. Think outside the box, she reminds herself.

In a flash a possible scenario presents itself. It's not something he's done but something he's forgotten. Yes, that could work. It would have to be something of major significance to her like… what? A milestone birthday perhaps? Daisy jots it down, then crosses it out. The wife would surely have mentioned that in advance. Silver wedding anniversary? Probably ages ago, thinks Daisy, assessing their ages to be around seventy. But a ruby wedding … that would work. Most men gave up counting long before fifty, didn't they? He's forgotten, so she's celebrating on her own; with him but without him. Daisy puts her pen down and sits back, confident that she can build a short story around that.

She watches the woman struggle into her coat and scrabble in her bag for her purse, as her husband strolls off in the direction of the gents with his hands in his pockets.

After they've left, she orders pizza and salad and eats slowly while trying to decide if her story will allow him to make the connection before the day is out. On balance she thinks not. She also wonders about the reality of their situation but decides that the fictional version is likely to be the more interesting.

CHAPTER 4

The F in Food, Fergus and InFuriating

※

Lavinia had been aware from the outset that Fergus was pernickety. However, it was not until the whole engagement, marriage and honeymoon thing was over that the complexity of his idiosyncrasies came to light.

They had returned from a frugal fortnight on French campsites having survived, to a great extent, on bread and cheese, fruit and crème caramel – Lavinia's treat. The honeymoon over, they had settled themselves into the new two-up two-down semi they had scrimped and saved for and Lavinia was eager to flex her culinary skills on a celebratory Sunday lunch. Fergus had been enthusiastic and full of praise for her perfectly cooked lamb, the creamy mash and crispy roast potatoes, but he had stalled on his first mouthful of cabbage. Lavinia had cooked it carefully, steaming it in the modern way and serving it as her mother always had, finely chopped and dressed in butter and white pepper. Fergus' ferocious reaction took her by surprise, to the extent that she thought she might have accidentally poisoned him.

'What the hell have you done with the cabbage?' he spluttered as he gulped down an entire glass of water and poured another.

When the drama was over, it transpired that Fergus couldn't cope either with pepper or finely chopped cabbage, which was, he declared, 'forever falling off the fiddling fork.'

During the ensuing months, by way of multiple episodes of coughing, spluttering and gulping, Lavinia discovered Fergus was averse to almost all herbs, spices and condiments except salt. He wouldn't eat green peppers, pork or porridge. Sardines, mackerel and herring were off limits and shellfish made him sick.

After thirty years of pandering to Fergus' fads and fancies, Lavinia had become, in her opinion, one of the best plain cooks in the county. Nevertheless, the restrictions placed on her culinary flair still rankled and she would justify her bland cuisine, to any guests, with throwaway remarks and a martyr's smile.

'Of course, Fergus suffers with his stomach you

know. In the way some people do with their nerves. It's a constant battle.'

In recent weeks the situation had become even more irksome. Fergus was experiencing disturbed sleep and by association, so was Lavinia. Night after night he prowled between the bedroom and the bathroom, burping noisily, gulping water and slurping Gaviscon straight from the bottle. When she remonstrated with him about the inaccuracy of such doses and the undoubted contamination of the contents of the bottle, he reasoned he couldn't use a spoon because he didn't want to disturb her by switching on the light. Lavinia pleaded with him to consult a specialist. Fergus, however, was convinced that he knew the workings of his own system well enough to figure out a diagnostic plan for himself.

'If I go and see some flash Harry at the hospital, the first thing he'll do is stick a camera down my throat, just because he can.'

'Well at least you'd have some idea of what's going on down there,' Lavinia retorted.

Fergus was unmoved and Lavinia made no apology for removing herself into the spare room while he figured out his diagnostic plan.

His strategy amounted to his own version of an elimination diet.

First to be excluded was fat, a decision Fergus based on one terrible night following a large portion of apple pie with clotted cream. He instructed Lavinia to purchase skimmed milk and fat-free yoghurt and drew up a list, which he secured to the door of the fridge with a cupcake magnet. The list detailed the foods he was planning to boycott. When Lavinia read bacon, sausages, ham, cheese, fried eggs, chips, roasties, cakes, pastry and biscuits, and added them to her mental list of things that were routinely off limits, her heart sank.

The trial, for such it was in every sense, lasted three weeks without any discernible improvement in Fergus's gastric equilibrium.

Next, he turned his attention to lactose. Lavinia restocked the fridge with almond milk, lactose-free cheese and yoghurts. A week later she threw them all out. After one bowl of cereal, one cup of tea and one yogurt, lactose was off the hook purely on grounds of taste. Gluten was the next substance under scrutiny, all brands of gluten-free bread eventually being declared 'no better than cardboard'. Lavinia even unearthed the bread maker from the back of a cupboard and produced several gluten-free bricks before admitting defeat. She did however, make a delicious cranberry and pecan loaf for herself and bought Fergus some oatcakes.

Several weeks into the gluten-free phase they had occasion to stop at a motorway services, not a food outlet to pander to the likes of Fergus when compiling their *Lite Bite Selection*. Fergus was hungry and fractious.

Throwing the menu on the table, he growled, 'Oh, to hell with it,' and ordered two fried eggs on two slices of white toast and a jam doughnut. That night Fergus had the best sleep he'd had for months.

'Irrefutable proof,' he declared at breakfast the following morning. 'Fat and gluten are in the clear.'

Encouraged by such an unequivocal result, he pressed on with his investigations. During the ensuing weeks he eliminated, in turn, meat, apples, onions, coffee, chocolate, cheese and potatoes. All to no avail. Lavinia's brain, by this time, was scrambled. She felt unable to make any decisions about food or even about shopping. Her nights, no longer plagued by Fergus' activities, were now beset by disturbing dreams of rampant herbs and spices, culinary calamities and medical crises. Fergus' research was draining the very essence out of her. She was no longer interested in cooking anything at all and vehemently voiced her opinion that it was surely time to let Flash Harry have a go.

Fergus remained steadfast. 'One of these days something will give.'

When things eventually did take a different turn, it was not quite the definitive breakthrough Fergus had predicted, or what Lavinia had hoped for.

Fergus appeared on the threshold of Lavinia's bedroom one morning, bearing two mugs of what Lavinia presumed was coffee and an expression altogether too cheery for the hour.

'I've come to a decision,' he announced.

'Do you mean about seeing a specialist?'

'No, no no. Not about that. I've decided that the problem is more likely to be about water, or rather, the lack of it. We need to drink lots more water.'

'We?' hissed Lavinia.

'Well, yes. I thought you might like to join me. I have read all about it on the iPad and it really would do us both so much good. Huge benefits apparently. So I've brought you some hot water with lemon to start the day. I've also filled up the big jug. I thought we could leave it on the worktop as a reminder during the day.'

Lavinia stared at Fergus, her lips tightly clamped as she fought, with only partial success, to control her emotions before she spoke.

'It seems to have escaped your notice that I already drink several glasses of water every day from the filter jug that has sat beside the kettle for at least two years. However, if you feel the need to commission your own personal jug, that's fine by me. But don't expect me to match you glass for glass just because you've got a bee in your bonnet about dehydration all of a sudden. It's one step too far. This so-called investigation of yours has ruled our lives for months and you are no further forward than at the start.'

'But Lavinia, I thought …'

'No more theories, Fergus.'

Lavinia swung her legs out of bed, grabbed her dressing gown from the chair and glancing at the mug of hot water on the bedside cabinet she said,

'You can drink that one as well if you like. It really isn't my sort of thing. I'm going to put the coffee pot on. And incidentally,' she called from the top of the stairs, 'you might want to check out what the iPad has to say about alcohol as a gastric irritant… just a thought.'

CHAPTER 5

Fergus Does Some Shopping

※

It was Thursday, the day of the weekly shop. Fergus hated shopping as much, if not more than, cutting the grass. But since he and Lavinia had both retired, she had insisted that the regular trek to the supermarket should be a shared chore. Fergus realised he was out of his depth when she said, 'Considering the amount of time and effort I have had to put in to comply with your dietary whims and foibles over the years, the very least you can do is to help with the purchase, transport and heavy lifting involved.'

No get-out clauses in that one, Fergus calculated. He

acquiesced. It was only once a week after all. However, it didn't stop him grumbling about it.

Even before the white noise, the inconsiderate shoppers, the fractious kids, and the constant announcements of the day's bargains kicked in, there was the car park to contend with. Fergus purposely drove to the furthest point from the door in order to avoid the little yellow carts manned by pushy men with challenging beady eyes.

'Vash-an-palish very quick! Ten pound only sir madam!'

'Worse than bloody seagulls after your sandwich at the beach,' declared Fergus.

On this particular Thursday, he was incensed by the fact that the vash-an-palishers had all relocated to *his* end of the car park. After locking the car, he strode off, avoiding eye contact and leaving Lavinia to deliver the 'not today thank you' with a smile.

Things continued to conspire against Fergus. When an old friend of Lavinia's hailed her by the trolley store, he groaned inwardly. Experience told him this would take some time. Summoning his jovial side from his boots he managed, 'How nice to see you. It's been a while Barbara. Keeping well, I hope? George okay is he? Oh good, very good.' He eased the bags for life from under Lavinia's arm and took the list out of her hand.

'I'll go and make a start, shall I? So you two can have a chat ... no rush. Regards to George, Barbara.'

He swiftly released a trolley from the stack, flung the bags in the bottom with the list and sallied forth into Fruit and Veg. Fergus reckoned he'd have it all sorted and packed in the car by the time the two women had put the world back on its axis. He hummed a bit of the William Tell overture as he made for apples.

It was at this point that Fergus' persistent refusal to actively engage with the business of shopping began to cause problems. As a general rule he drove the trolley while Lavinia filled it. He did a lot of tutting at folks who abandoned trollies to go on a search or parked them at forty-five degrees to study E numbers on tinned peas with absolutely no regard to the flow of traffic along the aisles.

The list said 'Jazz apples'. To Fergus, one apple was much like another, apart from the green ones, and it was a pest having to read all the labels. On then to bananas. He couldn't recall the last time he'd seen those in the fruit bowl and there was an enormous choice. Apart from size, they all looked the same. 'A banana is a banana' he muttered, chucking a huge bunch of organic ones in the trolley.

Blueberries. What the hell were those? He couldn't find them, so he looked for bilberries instead, assuming Lavinia had misspelt it, and then asked a young man who was struggling with a palette load of cauliflower.

'No bilberries mate. We got blueberries. Next aisle. With the grapes and soft fruit stuff.'

Fergus winced at the raw mateyness of youth. The cauliflower had looked very good though. He checked, but it wasn't on the list. Blueberries came in very small packs. He had no idea what she could be planning to do with them, but was certain one wouldn't be enough, so he put in three and went in search of spinach. The cauliflower popped into his mind as he rifled through assorted plastic bags of green leaves. He wasn't that keen on spinach, so he nipped back to choose a big cauli along with some freshly dug Cornish potatoes, which weren't on the list either. It did occur to Fergus that there was hardly enough veg in the trolley to last a week, but Lavinia was a very organised shopper so he reckoned she must have thought it through and pushed on into Fresh Meat.

Chicken was their default Sunday roast, had been for years. It was a meal he really looked forward to. He wasn't fussed about the cold cut the following day and put up with the fricassee to use up what was left, but thankfully the biryani and the stroganoff were now distant memories

Fergus checked the list. 'Chicken' was there, but he noticed she had bracketed breasts and thighs alongside. His thoughts immediately shot off, without his permission, to a place he seldom visited anymore, and he caught himself grinning as he selected two packs of plump, organic chicken breasts and two of chunky thighs. Shopping wasn't so bad after all.

Lavinia normally sailed past the oils, picking her usual bottle as she went by, but the sight of the vast array on offer stopped Fergus in his tracks. He wasn't sure what her regular bottle looked like, but he was captivated by the subtle colours and shapes on display. He took himself on a virtual tour of Spain, Italy and Greece before selecting a rich yellow olive oil from Italy. The plain glass bottle had a levered stopper with a rubber washer that reminded him of pop bottles in his youth. Had he looked at the price, it would have provoked an acute attack of tutting.

'Clover' and 'Elmlea Double' were puzzling. To Fergus they sounded rather horticultural. He decided she must have put them on the wrong list, so without further ado he crossed them out. Luxury Swiss hot chocolate caught his eye and found its way into the trolley en route to the bakery, but coffee did not.

He located their usual loaf, but then noticed the list said 'honey' instead of marmalade and on this point, he agreed with it. It would make a nice change. He chose a jar shaped like a beehive and forged ahead into Cereals. His hand was already reaching for Bran-flakes when he read 'Corn'. Lavinia hadn't mentioned changing his breakfast and she rarely made mistakes. She had obviously been experiencing some kind of a 'moment' when compiling this list. The bag of oats added weight to his theory. They hadn't had porridge for years, principally because he didn't like it. However, with some honey and a big dollop of double cream, Fergus thought it might be worth giving it another go, so he nipped back to Dairy and put a large pot of 'extra thick double' into the trolley.

He checked his watch. She was taking ages over her chat, but he was almost done, just two more things to find; both of which caused him to wonder if Lavinia was in the throes of a mental hiccup. He looked at the list and then looked again. It definitely said 'cat food'.

She surely wasn't planning on acquiring a cat without discussing it. Or was she? No, that was ridiculous. It was most likely for the old lady down the lane who couldn't get out much but did have a cat. Fergus didn't want to appear stingy by opting for the cheapest, so he chose a pack of six that was halfway between basic and Whiskas. No wonder she didn't want to carry it, he thought. It weighed a ton.

By this time the fun was wearing off.

'This is a bit much,' he muttered to himself as he ventured tentatively into the women's section of the Pharmacy. 'She should be doing this!'

He had no idea what women's disposable razors looked like and feeling acutely uncomfortable, he grabbed a huge bottle of body wash as if to validate his presence in the unfamiliar aisle before making haste to the checkout. She would have to buy her own personal stuff. Only so much a man could do, he thought.

In the queue he mused on the idea of Lavinia having a bristly chin. He hadn't noticed anything of that nature, but then the 'up close and personal' side of things had taken a bit of a dive since she'd decided to sleep in the spare room. Not that it was a problem. He quite enjoyed having his own space.

Fergus suddenly felt quite weary. It had all taken longer than he had anticipated. Lavinia still hadn't appeared, and he was more than a little put out because this last bit was quite tiresome. However, the cashier, aware that he was on his own, put things through slowly, giving him time to pack.

Lavinia showed up just as he was putting his card away.

'Good gracious, you've finished already! I must have been chatting for ages.'

Fergus grunted. Rattled by the cost of his purchases, he was trying to work out how he had spent so much more than usual for what looked like quite a bit less.

'Well, yes, I did think you'd catch up a bit sooner, but never mind now. Let's just get all this in the car and go home for a coffee.'

Fergus couldn't actually recall buying coffee, but assumed he must have done.

He carried the bags inside and began unpacking onto the kitchen table, while Lavinia busied herself filling the kettle and preparing mugs. Turning round to help sort out and put away, she gasped at the array of items on the table.

'Fergus! What on earth is all this? We've got the wrong shopping. How in heaven's name did you manage that without noticing?'

He thought she was joking at first, but the look on her face soon put him right.

'Don't be ridiculous Lavinia. I followed the list you gave me. Well, apart from one or two little extras.'

He scrabbled in his pocket for the proof.

'The only things I didn't get were your flippin' disposable razors. I felt very awkward looking for those. You'll have to get them yourself next time. Oh, and the spinach. Couldn't find it.'

'Fergus, I have no idea what you are rambling on about. I don't use disposable razors. Nor do we have a cat as far as I am aware.'

After smoothing out the crumpled piece of paper from his pocket, Fergus slapped it down on the table with confidence.

'Your list.'

Lavinia picked it up and spent a moment or two studying it before she looked up at Fergus.

'We have been married for forty years,' she said slowly.

'I would have thought that was long enough for you to recognise my handwriting. I didn't write this list, Fergus. I don't know where you got it, but it was most probably left in the trolley by a previous shopper. You really are an old fool sometimes, but I don't understand why you didn't twig that most of this is not what we usually buy.'

Fergus was struggling to rearrange his expression to something appropriate.

'I thought… well I… oh, it's of no importance what I thought.'

He saw that Lavinia was smiling. She had switched off the kettle and was pouring two mugs of milk into a pan.

'At a guess, I'd say you probably thought I was losing the plot.'

Fergus huffed and fluffed his denial.

'Anyway,' she said, 'since it's going to be an interesting week food wise, we'll start with a mug of this exotic Swiss hot chocolate and then, I'm afraid you are going to have to go back to the shop for some eggs, more vegetables and toilet rolls. Oh, and some of our usual coffee please.'

CHAPTER 6

Storm in a Quick Wash

※

Lavinia

Lavinia blamed Fergus' mother for many things and had set about retraining him within weeks of their marriage, with varying degrees of success. It had been an uphill struggle, but he no longer kept cotton handkerchiefs in his pockets to double up as dipstick wipes or paintbrush cleaners and he now routinely folded his socks in pairs before flinging them in the direction of the laundry basket. He had, finally, accepted that it was his job to empty the kitchen bin, although he regularly left it until one more item of rubbish would cause a health alert. Had Fergus been a dog, Lavinia mused, he would have been a feisty terrier with its own agenda. Biddable and compliant while you are watching but if you are not – anything goes!

This was very much the case with washing up. Lavinia had been taught as a child to wash the glasses first, followed by the knives, then the least messy dishes and remaining cutlery before the heavy-duty plates and pans. This system was greatly simplified by intelligent stacking beforehand. Dirty plates and pots were always rinsed or soaked and given a final rinse under the tap.

Lavinia's routine was a constant source of domestic friction. Fergus proclaimed it long-winded and totally unnecessary. Lavinia found his approach, at best, slapdash and occasionally hazardous to health. Once, for sheer devilment, Fergus cited his farmer friend, who regularly offered his plate to the dog for what he laughingly called a 'pre-wash' before rinsing it under the tap and leaving it to drain. A system that was, Fergus claimed, both elegantly simple and ecologically sound. Lavinia was appalled.

'That is positively medieval,' she said. 'Just think of the bugs.'

'Never done old Charlie any harm,' replied Fergus. 'Or the dog for that matter.'

The question of a dishwasher arose when Lavinia's oven died and 'oven repair man' declared it a write off. Being a man of vision, with a vested interest in white goods, he redesigned Lavinia's kitchen over a cup of her excellent coffee and a slice of the moribund oven's last date and walnut loaf. She was very taken with his idea of the double oven, wall-mounted microwave, integral fridge freezer and dishwasher, not to mention the pullout pantry cupboard. Looking at her kitchen through 'oven repair man's' eyes, it became obvious that it was well overdue for a make-over and she put the proposal to Fergus.

He almost choked on his *pain au chocolat* when she aired her plans, and his wallet went into a spasm when it heard the estimated cost. Lavinia could see she faced a mountain of opposition.

Fergus

Fergus quite liked washing up despite the squabbles it provoked when he sabotaged Lavinia's systems, but he rarely did it any more as he always seemed to be allocated the tea towel. This was tedious, because it involved putting things away and thus falling foul of the cupboard arrangements. He failed to see why mugs had to be on the left and glasses on the right... or was it the other way round? Anyway, as long as they were in the cupboard it was his considered opinion that the sky wasn't going to fall.

Fergus' philosophy on household maintenance was equally pragmatic. It went something like this. If it's broken, first try to fix it. If that fails, call in a 'man who can'. If it's not broken, there is no problem. So to Fergus' way of thinking, Lavinia's kitchen had only one problem – a dead oven.

Electricity was beyond Fergus's field of expertise. Hence the man, who in this instance, couldn't fix it but had planted the idea in Lavinia's head that she required a completely new kitchen to solve the oven problem. Fergus argued his case.

'So, we need a new oven. Fine, we'll buy a new oven. But there is nothing wrong with the rest of the kitchen that a screwdriver and a lick of paint can't fix. I'll even paint it buttercup yellow if you like.'

Lavinia snorted. 'If we had a new kitchen, we could have a dishwasher.'

'There isn't room for a dishwasher and besides, you've already got one – me!'

'Yes, well, be that as it may, I would quite like a proper one. Then I wouldn't have to put up with your constant grumbling.'

'Lavinia, not only does the kitchen lack the space, it also lacks the necessary plumbing for a dishwasher.'

'My point exactly,' said Lavinia. 'If the kitchen is reorganised and appropriate plumbing is installed there will be room for a dishwasher.'

Fergus veered off into safer territory, as she had known he would eventually.

'What about the cost? We're talking about a hefty sum of money just because your oven is kaput.' The words were hardly out of his mouth when he spotted the trap he'd fallen into.

'Bugger,' he thought. 'Bugger, bugger, bugger.'

'Yes, I've been thinking about money,' continued Lavinia. 'Have you by any chance totted up your expenditure over the last few months?'

'No doubt you are about to enlighten me down to the last five pence.'

'Just an outline. I'm sure you can work out the detail. First there was the band saw you couldn't manage without. Then the pillar drill, because there was no point in having one without the other. Next came the heavy-duty shredder, the new lens for your camera and all the fencing for the paddock to contain someone else's horses because you don't want to mow it. That is aside from your ongoing expenditure on paints, brushes, canvasses, frames …'

Fergus groaned, took a white tissue out of the box on the table and waved it in submission.

Beko, the Dishwasher

'I am installed in very nice place, I think. Smart new kitchen with Zanussi fridge freezer and Neff double oven. The lady of the house, she called Lavinia by the way, she look a lot at Bosch dishwasher in showroom until I catch her eye. She like my price. Is good price for top of range you know. I very economic with water and electric and I not make many decibels. Lady's husband like price very much but I think he don't care about other excellent qualities.

After I am installed, lady sit at kitchen table and look at me and I know she like what she see. She read my booklet, every page. Then she open my door and put salt in place for salt. She take mugs and plates from sink and place carefully in top rack. Fry pan and milk pan she put at bottom and she use good quality wash tablet not cheap supermarket own brand. She know I am Beko dishwasher top of range. Oh yes, I will make her dishes sparkle. All is good. Nice lady, new kitchen and top of range fridge freezer. Shame she Zanussi but maybe lady buy Beko next time.

I have live here now for many weeks and I have learn a lot. My English is much better thank you and I have learn many new words. But some, I think, is better not to say, like words the man say if he very cross.

I love the lady. She have learn how to use all my programmes and she is very happy with Beko dishwasher. But the man, Mister Fergoose, is I think you say a 'pain in ze bum, yes?' He throw dishes in willy-nilly and then say bad word when beer glass come out streaky. He say to lady, 'This top of range dishwasher is waste of money.'

He no learning to stack right and he push my button too hard and too short so I not start. He refuse to learn push soft and hold two second. Is not difficult and sometimes he put all pots and pans on 'Quick Wash'. He don't care that water not hot enough for greasy pot. One day last week he lose temper and kick me. It was good job he only wear slipper or my body would have dent. Yes, Mister Fergoose upsets me quite a lot. I talk to Zanussi about it and she have help me make a plan. She say I must make protest like flood in kitchen. Of course, Beko dishwasher is not suppose to do that but I learn a trick or two in my home country and I know how. I wait till lady go out and then I make big flood. Mister Fergoose use many bad words I not heared before and he have to get mop and bucket. He tells lady to call Beko engineer and when he come to run diagnostic test, of course, he did not found problem. (Is no problem except Mister Fergoose!) He check all pipes and seals and tells lady must of been a flook. I never heared of flook but I don't think Beko top of range would have flook.

After engineer finished lady is very cross with Mister Fergoose. She even use his bad words. She say he must of bugger up Beko somehow. So he say, 'Fine, you can deal with dishes and dishwasher then.' He walk out and slam kitchen door.

I feel a little sorry for lady but is good result for Beko I think. No?

CHAPTER 7

Fergus Finds His Muse

For as long as Fergus could remember he had yearned to play a musical instrument. The feeling had persisted even when, after six tortuous months of piano lessons, his teacher, the buxom Miss Wissle, had told his mother, 'This boy does not have a single musical cell in his makeup'.

In his own defence Fergus later remarked, 'She was creepy. She was fat and sweaty, and she practically sat on my lap. *And* she hit my fingers with a huge wooden knitting needle.'

Miss Wissle's comments, however, persuaded Fergus' mother that there was no point in investing any further in her son's aspirations and the subject was closed.

After flirting briefly with the recorder at school and the harmonica in his free time, Fergus put his dreams on hold and launched himself into a career in the creative arts. By the time he and Lavinia had made their pact for life, he was happily involved in teaching the fundamentals of three-dimensional design to art students. Given their voracious appetites for originality and their belief that they could improve on the wheel, it was inevitable that musical instruments would come under scrutiny at some point. And so they did, rekindling Fergus' dormant desire to play something – anything.

The bright young things of the eighties concentrated on form, function and aesthetics as required by their course and when their 'New Age' instruments were finished they made music. Fergus was immensely proud of their achievements and deeply jealous of their innate musicality.

Over the ensuing decade Lavinia, who had put her own passion for food on hold while she tried to accommodate Fergus' idiosyncratic digestive system, became a silent witness to his growing obsession with finding *his* instrument. Keyboards and strings were quickly eliminated as too complex. The legacy of Miss Wissle's savage knitting needle endured.

'It's not that I aspire to any level of virtuosity,' he told Lavinia. 'I'd just like to be able to knock out a couple of shit-kicking tunes for my own amusement. Nothing complicated.'

Lavinia groaned. She was not familiar with shit-kicking music, but it sounded a million miles from Beethoven's *Für Elise* or the *Pastoral Symphony*. She did not share Fergus' belief that everybody could play *something*, an opinion she based on his tuneless whistle, his flat singing voice and his inability to master the foxtrot or the cha cha. She was convinced that this madcap idea would eventually fizzle out, so she paid little attention to the steady accumulation of instruments in Fergus's studio. He was a collector by nature, a rescuer of books, pebbles, keys, chairs, old gardening implements, in fact of almost anything that had made it out of the past. A few musical bits and pieces merely added piquancy to his collection.

The clapped-out 1950s guitar was lovingly restored, restrung and relegated to a hook on the wall. A decrepit banjo was equally revered and similarly abandoned. A 17th century ocarina languished among tubes of oil paint on the windowsill. A nineteenth century flageolet reclined in the corner of a shelf with a modern bass recorder. All had auditioned for the role of Fergus' muse, and all had failed. The last contender had been an enormous didgeridoo, an instrument often called 'the drone pipe', and after hearing the excruciating tones emanating from Fergus' studio, Lavinia could well understand why. She renamed the offending instrument a dirgeridoo.

Not one to give up without a fight, Fergus enlisted the help of a YouTube video to learn how to control his breath. Lavinia subsequently endured several weeks of keeping one eye on the TV and the other on Fergus as he practised breathing techniques. His eyes popped and his reddened cheeks bulged, giving the impression of a man either drowning or in the throes of a cardiovascular accident.

When she could no longer stand the tension she said, 'Fergus this can't be doing you any good. You are too old to start learning to breathe like an Aborigine. You'll give yourself, or me, a heart attack.'

He took a huff and disappeared into the kitchen to breathe unobserved. However, the didgeridoo kept its secrets to itself and Fergus' passion waned as he notched up another failure and sank into a deep depression.

His gloom set in with the onset of winter. Fergus' usual irrepressible bounce was deflated, and it seemed to Lavinia that he and his Stressless chair had merged into one. He didn't go for his paper. He didn't read or doodle in his sketch pad. He rarely went out except to the bin, and his studio remained locked and cold.

Lavinia suggested he should light the stove and listen to music out there for a change of scene. 'You could tidy the place up a bit while you're not actively involved in anything,' she offered.

Fergus responded with a glare, folded his arms across his chest, closed his eyes and retreated into his head.

Lavinia was at her wits' end. She thought he might need some pills, but couldn't see a way of persuading him to see a doctor. She had been down that route once before, albeit for different reasons. It had been spectacularly unsuccessful. Fergus was a man who didn't take kindly to being pushed. Diversionary tactics were required, and an idea presented itself to Lavinia from an unexpected quarter.

She had shut herself in the kitchen with a pile of ironing and Woman's Hour. She found Jenni Murray's voice quite soothing, although she was decidedly unimpressed with some of the programme's recent topics. The LGBT movement for instance, which was, in her opinion, a minority interest. Child grooming in Telford (wherever that was) and most recently, the life and times of the winner of the Great British Sewing Bee.

'Oh, for heaven's sake!' she shouted at the radio. 'Whatever happened to informed content? This is just tittle tattle.'

She was composing a letter of complaint to the BBC in her head when the word 'depression' caught her attention. She put down the iron to listen. The phrase *Be careful what you wish for* would come hurtling in her direction much later, but at that moment she saw the glimmer of a solution to breaking the impasse around her gloomy husband.

On the day of an international rugby match, Lavinia roasted a chicken, Fergus' favourite dinner. For dessert she made an apricot pudding with oaty topping and home-made custard. When they were tidying up before the start of the match she said, 'Do you remember having an African drum ages and ages ago? Did you chuck it out or give it away?'

Fergus paused with his hand on the cutlery drawer.

'It was a Djembe. I put it in the charity shop, and it was gone the next day. Whatever made you think of that? It was way back.'

'Oh, I don't know. Something I heard on Radio Four, I think. A neuroscientist somewhere has come up with a theory about drums being used to cheer people up. It's good for raising endorphins or some such.'

'Never really got the hang of drumming,' mused Fergus. 'Two left hands like two left feet, that's my problem.'

'Perhaps it wasn't the right kind of drum for you,' said Lavinia.

'Lots of different kinds apparently, even one-handed ones.'

Fergus hurrumphed. 'Those will be for the one-armed drummers I guess.'

'Oh, don't be ridiculous,' said Lavinia. 'They have to

have another hand to hold the thing! Go and watch your match.'

He threw the tea towel at her and disappeared into the sitting room.

Over the next couple of weeks Lavinia noticed subtle changes in Fergus' mood. He and his chair were still very much a couple, but the iPad had joined them. Fergus was awake more often. He had his earphones in, and every now and then Lavinia noticed his feet tapping. The Encyclopaedia of Musical Instruments came in from the studio. Lavinia said nothing, but she recognised the signs of an awakening passion. Confirmation came when Fergus returned from town with a broad grin on his face and brandishing what looked like a tambourine without jingles.

'It's a bodhran,' he informed her. 'Ancient Irish single-hand drum.'

Lavinia's eyebrows broadcast scepticism loud and clear.

'Obviously, this one isn't ancient,' said Fergus. 'It's a cheap imitation from China, but it will be okay for starters.'

Throughout the summer, with the assistance of Jonny 'Ringo' McFadden on YouTube, Fergus literally drummed the skin off his knuckles. When Lavinia complained about the number of rolls of Micropore tape he was using to wrap them up he switched to using bright green insulation tape, which he declared was 'far superior anyway.'

Fergus became a bit like an outside cat. He appeared only at mealtimes and sloped off again after he'd been fed. In the evenings, sitting in his Stressless chair, he drummed with a pencil on a hard-backed book. Lavinia turned the volume up a notch on the TV and tried to ignore him.

Inevitably, the cheap Chinese instrument soon failed to satisfy, and a handmade drum arrived from a small company in Wales. This one had a more mellow tone, she was informed. Next came an enormous instrument made to order by an old man in the Hebrides. The arrival of this new drum prompted Fergus to give his fingers some respite and he began experimenting with drumsticks. Not regular, run of the mill drumsticks of course. These were lovingly carved from leftovers of exotic wood which Fergus had unearthed in the studio, and they racked up the decibels considerably.

Around the same time, Fergus extended his YouTube excursions into Europe, where he discovered Brendan White in Holland. Brendan, a renowned player and maker of the Rolls Royce of bodhrans, became Fergus' new best friend and he soon wanted a Brendan White drum. There was an email exchange, one drummer to another, buddies now and in due course the crème-de-la-creme of single hand drums arrived. Fergus was ecstatic.

Lavinia not so much. She was beginning to regret setting this particular top spinning, and with good reason.

The 'Brendan White' turned out to be somewhat delicate in character. It was not happy with the humidity in the studio. Particularly since by now, it was mid-autumn and much colder than usual. Fergus took to bringing it into the house in the evenings to prevent it going flat. Occasionally he would say, 'I'm just popping up to the back bedroom for a minute. There's something I want to try on the drum. Won't be long. I'll close all the doors.'

Lavinia forced a smile and increased the volume on the TV.

I should have seen this coming she thought, and it wasn't long before the 'just popping', evolved into a regular thing after dinner. It was then only a matter of time before it became too cold in the studio for Fergus too. He and his drums came in for the winter. The noise factor in the sitting room was low level and could be masked by music or the television. In the kitchen, however, it was the equivalent of standing under a railway bridge as express trains went over. Lavinia found herself looking back wistfully at the previous winter when Fergus had hardly stirred out of his chair.

Jenni Murray has a lot to answer for, she thought. But on the other hand, Fergus was happier now than he had been for ages. The next time she was in town she selected a pair of top-quality noise cancelling earphones and didn't even wince when they told her the price.

CHAPTER 8

Lavinia Embarks on a Creative Journey

Fergus' retirement had swivelled Lavinia's life onto a different axis. She had already spent a couple of years adjusting to her own altered status and had set up new routines and systems to keep herself occupied and stimulated. The Book Group focused her reading, and it was worth going just for the cake, supplied by Marjorie, who regularly took first prize at W. I. events. Theatre Group was only three or four times a year, but they had seen some very entertaining productions and it was always a good night out. At home she had embarked on a long-term project to transform their labour-intensive garden into something more manageable into their dotage. She was never idle, and for the most part she was content.

Inevitably, when they were both permanently orientated around the homestead the dynamics changed again. Lavinia was reluctant to admit it, but she was a smidgen envious of Fergus' dedication to his most recent passion, which had shown no sign of fizzling out. Fergus and his muse had become an item and Lavinia had become a drum widow. Generally, she would describe him as a grumbler and a bumbler, doing a bit of this and that and not a lot of the other. The new fired-up Fergus left her feeling somewhat adrift in her own world, and she was surprised to find herself more than a little lonely.

Fergus spent hours practising in the back bedroom during the day and, in the evenings, used his own headphones to block out Lavinia's TV programmes while he watched Jonny 'Ringo' McFadden's tutorials on YouTube. Over breakfast he waxed lyrical about Jonny's virtuosity and updated Lavinia on his own laborious progress. Occasionally he would appear with the bodhran and ask, 'Have you got a minute to listen to this and tell me what you think?'

Lavinia listened and told him what she thought, but she couldn't believe she had anything valid to contribute, given that she was not on the same wavelength as Jonny Ringo. Fergus, however, seemed quite content with her comments and trundled off to continue his practice.

It was Lavinia's best friend Helen who pointed out that she was losing track of her own life by becoming ensnared in Fergus'.

'It's getting you down darling. I can tell,' she said.

She and Lavinia were chatting over a coffee in La Bamba after a shopping spree.

'You need to break out; do your own thing. Pottery class, belly dancing or Couch to 5k!'

Lavinia exploded at the last suggestion. 'I rather think my running days are over, don't you?'

Helen gave her an appraising look. 'Folks older than you have done it. You're not in bad shape but I know what you mean. It's the knees darling. Mine are shot too. Actually, you'd probably enjoy something a bit more brain orientated, like Italian or... or... creative writing! What about that? I bet you've got loads of stories to tell.'

'Oh, get away with you,' laughed Lavinia. 'Me and the rest of the world I should think.'

'Well, at least promise me you'll think about it. You need to do something for your inner self and to hell with old Fergus.'

'I promise,' said Lavinia.

The idea of learning a foreign language from scratch was quite daunting. If there had been a French Improvers' class she might have been tempted, but Beginners' Spanish or

Italian sounded like a lot of hard work. Creative Writing was a daytime course and just eight weeks.

'Bring a pen and a pad and discover your voice in a friendly, supportive environment,' it said on the website.

Lavinia signed up. She could manage eight weeks.

The first session was nerve-racking. It was decades since she'd been in a learning environment. Some in the group had been before and were quite vociferous. Lavinia retreated into 'church mouse' mode, not wishing to make a fool of herself, but they were a friendly group. The tutor was kind and encouraging about her first hesitant efforts on the old shorthand pad she had grabbed from the bureau on the first morning.

By the end of the third session Lavinia's confidence had grown and she began to enjoy the classes and the challenges. As she strolled back to her car, contemplating the homework assignment she had been set on 'Character Development', it occurred to her that if she was going to develop characters, they ought to inhabit a designated notebook and, with extraordinary synchronicity, Paperway was the next shop she saw. Lavinia glanced at her watch. She had plenty of time to pop in and choose something.

Paperway was a shop she used only rarely, if she needed a special card for someone, so she was surprised to find that notebooks were not only abundant but that the available choice was almost overwhelming.

I need to establish criteria, she thought. She went to stand in front of the birthday cards so as to appear focused and not like a somewhat fazed elderly lady. Which is exactly what you are, she reminded herself as she gathered her thoughts.

Lines or blank pages? Lines would help to keep her on track.

Hardback or soft? Her favourite place to scribble was on her lap, so it would have to be hardback.

Spiral bound? Yes, because you could tear pages out without the whole damn thing falling apart.

Size? This was crucial. Not too small obviously; no room to flow. A5 would fit in her handbag, but she recalled that most of the group used A4. Well, she could always buy a bigger bag.

Lavinia refocused on the cards and on a rabbit with huge ears that appeared to be grinning at her. So far so good, she thought. Just the colour to decide on and possibly a pattern.

Her characters, when she got round to developing them, would, she hoped, be worthy of something more than the basic. Definitely not black or navy. Pink or lilac screamed teenage girl. Green reminded her of her mother, who would have spluttered into her Martini at the very idea of Lavinia writing anything more substantial than a shopping list. She winked at the rabbit and moved tentatively towards notebooks with patterned covers.

It crossed Lavinia's mind that three weeks before, she would have quite happily picked up an A4 jotter in the supermarket, and she wondered what had happened to change a basic notepad into an item of significance.

She glanced at her watch. Goodness, she had been in the shop for ages and her time was nearly up in the carpark. Her choice was going to have to be in the hands of serendipity. Her fingers alighted on a silver-grey cover with a dark blue image of an antique inkwell and quill on the front. Underneath, in copperplate script, was the word *Inspiration*. It was perfect.

Lavinia made her purchase and hastened back to the car, her mind buzzing.

Having let serendipity out of its box, she allowed it to take her to the garden centre instead of going straight home to make Fergus his midday sandwich. She hadn't given him a thought for hours. It was quite refreshing. She made a beeline for the café, ordered a cappuccino and instead of her usual toasted teacake, a large slice of triple-layer coffee and walnut cake with buttercream icing. She chose a table in a corner by the window from where she was able to cast a critical eye over her surroundings both inside and out. Could her characters be found here, she wondered?

Lost in her musings, she used her fingers to chase the last sticky cake crumbs around her plate, licked them, and immediately looked around, horrified, in case anyone had witnessed her lapse in table etiquette. She delicately wiped her mouth and fingers on the paper napkin to make amends, if only to herself.

She withdrew her new notebook from its bag, admired the front cover and opened it at the first page. It stared blankly at her. She was itching to make a significant mark, to claim it as her own. All words were suddenly absent, gone into hiding, fearful of insignificance or wary of judgment. She fumbled in her handbag for her pen and slowly took off the top, playing for time. Very deliberately she wrote her name in the top left-hand corner of the inside cover: *Lavinia Moreton*. With a wry smile she remembered claiming books in a similar fashion as a child when she wrote '*This book belongs to Lavinia Dawson. True.*'

That blank page was still challenging her. She held her pen over the top line and wrote the date in longhand. It seemed to Lavinia to be an important day. She cast her mind back to the first class when the tutor had told them, 'Just put your pen on the paper and see where it takes you.'

This was completely new territory for Lavinia. She did like to know where she was going or in most instances, where Fergus was going as she tagged along. She had never been one for magical mystery tours. Briefly, she considered whether she should have opted for the Spanish course, and her spirits tumbled. That's the cake, she told herself, big sugar rush and then a drop. I should know better by now. She decided to have another coffee.

In the queue at the service counter, Lavinia idly watched the antics of the flamboyant barista, king of the coffee machine, as he juggled with cups and nozzles. His name badge said 'Luigi' and he was sounding off like a firecracker to an older woman who was retaliating in what sounded like Italian. She was obviously cross with him about something, and Lavinia wondered how they both came to be in a garden centre in the middle of Shropshire.

She paid for her coffee and Luigi said he would bring it across to her when it was ready. From her table she watched him sashay towards her, coffee on a tray held with one hand at shoulder height. He was handsome and slim, and he had now swapped his scowl for a wide Mediterranean smile. 'Cappuccino, madam,' he said, setting the tray down with a flourish. 'Made especially for you. Enjoy!'

Lavinia beamed at him. 'Thank you very much.'

She sipped through the warm chocolate covered foam and picked up her pen. Underneath the date she wrote ... Luigi, Italian, young, fiery, and charming. Making coffee in middle England... what is he doing here? Who is the older woman? Why is she angry with him?

Lavinia smiled. She had found a character. Only time would tell if Luigi was *the* character. But she had breached the barrier of that first page, and it felt oh so good.

CHAPTER 9

Just Another Thursday

Lavinia felt she and Fergus had glided through life like a pair of aged swans, their rhythms and patterns fixed by years of common usage. Inevitably, feathers got ruffled sometimes, but even so, what Fergus thought of as compatibility and she regarded as forbearance had been finely tuned over the years.

One Thursday they emerged from their respective bedrooms, each with one foot still in the grasp of the night. Silently they danced through their choreographed bathroom ritual. Lavinia in and out. Fergus in and out. Lavinia in again for final touches, hairspray, moisturiser and the lightest touch of lipstick. Someone had once told her that if life ever became challenging, one could remedy it by smiling into a mirror, so, Lavinia had incorporated a lipstick smile in her daily practice.

'Morning!' she trilled to Fergus as they met at the top of the stairs. 'Sleep well?'

Fergus grunted.

Lavinia made the coffee and set out breakfast while Fergus checked out the news on his iPad.

'Shopping today?' she asked. They always did the shopping on Thursdays.

Fergus nodded and continued chomping through his muesli. Lavinia toyed with Greek yogurt, blueberries, and seeds and savoured the first coffee of the day. She liked to take her mornings at a gentle pace.

'I'll go and get the car out,' said Fergus as soon as he'd finished. He was oblivious, even after decades, to the fact that Lavinia had things to do before leaving the house. The dishwasher had to be emptied. The bird feeder had to be filled. She had to check her hair, pop to the loo, and locate her list.

Fergus was parked outside the gate with the engine off, tapping on the steering wheel, when Lavinia finally emerged with three 'bags for life' tucked under one arm. The freezer bag swung from her wrist and her handbag flew open as she attempted to drop her keys in while shutting the gate. She flung her shopping bags into the back and collapsed into the passenger seat as Fergus started the engine.

'Whatever do you find to do between me getting the car out and you getting in it?' he grumbled. 'I've been sitting here for ages.'

'The same sort of things you have to do the minute your dinner is ready, I imagine,' retorted Lavinia.

Fergus gave her one of his looks, stamped on the accelerator and shot off down the lane, to rapid-fire beeps of protest from the car, as Lavinia struggled to fasten her seatbelt.

'What's the rush?' she asked.

'No rush' said Fergus, slamming the car into third as it growled up the hill. Lavinia sighed and wished she could manage the weekly shop on her own.

At the store, Fergus commandeered the trolley as usual and Lavinia darted back and forth, up and down the aisles, like a frantic blue tit feeding chicks. Frequently she found herself with an armful of cheese and yogurts or packets of pasta when Fergus and the trolley had disappeared, already advanced into tinned tomatoes and beans. Fergus was not a patient shopper.

When they finally approached the checkout, it amused Lavinia to watch him weighing up which one to go for, like a punter at the races. He chose the girl with the blonde ponytail, crimson lipstick and nails to match. She beamed at Fergus, ignored Lavinia, and put the shopping through at the rate of machine-gun fire. It was all Lavinia could do to pile it back into the trolley with some semblance of a system, because her fingers were still frozen after lingering in Meat, Dairy and Frozen Foods.

'I'm sure they've turned the heating down,' she muttered. 'It's like an ice box in here!'

Given a choice, Lavinia would have preferred to shop in Sainsbury's. There was greater variety, and the checkout system was more manageable. However, the wallet preferred the no-frills store and Fergus' taste for German beer clinched it. Lavinia couldn't object because she needed his help to lift bags, and he did come willingly most times. To compensate, every now and then, she went on a solo trip to her favourite supermarket for those few extra bits that the Germans obviously considered non-essential, like elderflower cordial, jumbo oats, and her preferred horseradish sauce with cream.

It was after they'd loaded the shopping into the boot that the usual Thursday excursion went 'off piste', so to speak.

'I'm going to nip into B&Q,' said Fergus. 'Save another journey. One or two bits I need in the studio.'

'Well, if we are going to do that, we may as well go to the retail park as well and that will save me another trip,' said Lavinia.

Fergus grunted, none too pleased at having his idea hijacked.

They were finally on their way home, after doing

Boots, Next and TK Maxx, when Lavinia exclaimed, 'Oh no! I've lost my gold ring.'

'What do you mean, lost?' said Fergus.

'Exactly that. It was on my finger and now it's not.'

'You probably forgot to put it on this morning.'

'I did not! I never take it off. I wear it to keep my other ring on because that is too big.'

'So where did you lose it?'

'I don't know. But it must have fallen off while we were shopping, obviously.'

'Do you want to go back?' said Fergus, momentarily taking his foot off the accelerator.

'Where to? It could be anywhere.'

'It's probably in with the shopping anyway,' said Fergus speeding up again.

'I loved that ring. It really is quite upsetting,' Lavinia said quietly.

'It's not your wedding ring is it?' asked Fergus, slowing down.

'No. I told you. I wear it on the other hand. Just goes to show how unobservant you are about things.'

Fergus didn't reply immediately as he was accelerating to beat a red light. Once through it, he said, 'Not such a big deal though is it? I mean... if it isn't your wedding ring.'

Lavinia took a deep breath and remained silent for a minute or two before responding.

'Do you know something Fergus? You can be an insensitive old sod at times.'

He had the grace to shoot her an apologetic glance, but she was looking out of the window.

The atmosphere in the car was arctic for the remainder of the journey. Lavinia retreated inside herself. It was such a pretty ring. She had no idea of its provenance, having found it at the bottom of her mother's jewellery box. It was old, certainly, and it looked as though it had been made especially for someone. Stylised flowers had been engraved on its wide surface. Lavinia had never seen another like it. She had often wondered whether there had perhaps been a scandal or a tragedy associated with the ring. It almost felt as if it had been hidden away on purpose. But it had spoken to her on some level. She had rescued it and now she had lost it. She was devastated, but also puzzled because the ring it was supposed to be safeguarding was still on her finger.

At home, Lavinia went through the shopping with forensic fervour. She searched the car and her pockets and tipped out her handbag and purse, giving them a good shake. Nothing; the ring really had gone.

She considered it very unlikely that it would be found. It might already be squashed flat under a tyre in a car park or at the bottom of a drain. Nevertheless, she had to try. So, armed with a list of numbers, she sat by the phone in the hall and contacted Customer Services in every shop she had visited.

No one was optimistic, particularly when she told them she had no idea where the ring might have slipped off her finger. She could do nothing more except hope. She removed the emerald eternity ring that had been her mother's and returned it to its box upstairs. Better safe than sorry. Her hand felt undressed without both rings, and the enduring presence of her snug-fitting wedding band offered no compensation at all.

'Any joy?' asked Fergus, handing her a mug of tea as she entered the kitchen. Lavinia shook her head.

'Chasing moonbeams if you ask me,' he said. 'Why is it so important anyway? Apart from its monetary value of course.'

'I don't know. It just is.'

'It's not as though it was a family heirloom. You don't know anything about it, do you?'

'Well it could be an heirloom,' said Lavinia. 'Just because I don't know doesn't mean it isn't and of course I'll never know. But it is very unusual, and I liked it – very much.'

Fergus huffed and stalked off to answer the phone.

'It's for you,' he called from the hall. 'Customer Service at Aldi.'

Lavinia held the phone like a piece of bone china as she listened.

'Yes, Lavinia Moreton speaking.' She held her breath.

Fergus heard her say 'That's wonderful. Thank you so much. No, no I'll come this afternoon. I'll come now in fact.'

She came back into the kitchen smiling broadly.

'Someone found it on the floor by the checkout. It must have fallen off when we were packing because my fingers were so cold. I'm going back to collect it now.'

'Now? But it's lunchtime!'

'Oh, I'm much too excited for lunch,' said Lavinia as she picked up the car keys and her handbag. 'There's enough food for a week here Fergus. I'm sure you'll find something to eat. I'll see you later.'

CHAPTER 10

A Weekend Break

Whenever Lavinia raised the subject of holidays, Fergus appeared to go deaf. She was well aware that he had perfected a technique for selecting the mute option on certain conversations, and especially those that involved his wallet. Fergus had never been keen on vacations. There was too much hanging about in airports, too much traffic on the roads, too much weather at sea and too many people everywhere. He was, in effect, wedded to his own pillow, his own bed and his Stressless chair. Lavinia sublimated her desires for a change of scene with solo forays into the wider world, meeting friends in her various groups and trawling her favourite shops for bargains. For her, there was nothing quite like a good shopping spree for raising her spirits.

Fergus wasn't really a sociable creature. He met up with his few good friends only occasionally, on a one-to-one basis, for a pint and a chinwag. So when he announced that his old school friend Mac, who farmed sheep just beyond Buxton, had invited him for the weekend, Lavinia was delighted.

Initially Fergus seemed quite taken with the idea, but as the weekend approached he became increasingly gloomy at the prospect.

'I'm not sure I really want to go,' he said. 'It's a long way in this weather.'

'It is only raining, Fergus.'

'I know, but his wife is away, and he's got the shearer coming on Saturday so it will be a bit frantic, if I know him.'

'Well, all the more reason to go, I would say,' countered Lavinia. 'You can give him a bit of support. It's only Derbyshire for God's sake, not the outback! Two old guys together, you can have a good rattle about past times.'

Lavinia could see her own tentative plans for a quiet weekend *sans* Fergus evaporating before they'd even fully formed. She piled on the pressure.

'I could roast a chicken for you to take with you if you like and I'll make a big fruit cake. I seem to remember Mac used to rave about my cakes. I'm sure it will do you good to have a break and shake your feathers. You've been stuck here for weeks with me and that drum upstairs.'

By eight-thirty on Friday morning Fergus was on his way, the chicken, the fruit cake and two bottles of decent French Merlot safely stowed in the boot.

Lavinia heaved a sigh of relief, made a fresh pot of coffee and sat down to plan her day.

I'll get all the chores done first thing, she thought. Then I'll go out.

Starting upstairs, she stripped the beds and turned the mattresses. Somehow, beds led to sorting out the airing cupboard which, she discovered, was long overdue. The bathroom cabinet caught her eye next, so she gave that a spring clean too. By this time it was pouring with rain and there was no chance of putting the sheets out for a blow. They would have to go on the airer in the conservatory, but she had to contend with Fergus' random storage techniques in order to extricate it from the bogey hole under the stairs.

With an aching back from bending double, Lavinia stopped for a coffee and considered the pile of stuff now in a heap on the hall carpet. Most of it could go in the recycling, which was Fergus' department. She moved it into the back porch, for his attention when he returned. The porch was already cluttered with things that Fergus had rescued from the recycling on the assumption that they would 'come in handy'. The fifty or so small foil pots for instance, and as many yogurt pots. Lavinia left five of each and hid the rest under that week's detritus.

When she finally looked at the time it was half past three. She hadn't had any lunch and it was too late to 'do' anything. She made a pot of Earl Grey and a round of cheese on toast and collapsed on the sofa with her memory foam cushion and some Ibuprofen.

A couple of hours later she was woken by the persistent ringing of the telephone. It was Fergus letting her know he had arrived. Glancing at her watch, she saw it was almost six-thirty. Peeved that she had allowed household trivia to claim her day, she responded somewhat uncharitably to his call.

'I think there would have been a panda car here before now if you'd been in a pile-up on the A38. But thanks for ringing. No, I haven't had dinner yet. I've been busy.'

Lavinia was too tired to cook. She heated some soup and one of Fergus' bread rolls that cook in ten minutes. 'Would I Lie to You?' was on the television. The mock furious banter between the team captains always made her smile and she felt better after she'd eaten. Tomorrow, she vowed, she would do something for herself.

On Saturday morning, Lavinia slept late. She put this down to the fact that she had worked quite hard the previous day and to the eerie quiet in the house without Fergus. For a man who maintained radio silence until he'd consumed at least one cup of coffee and a bowl of muesli, he actually made an extraordinary amount of noise. He coughed and cleared and blew with gusto to set himself up for the day. He slammed the shower door in and out and huffed and puffed himself dry. He dropped things on the floor and into the basin and his gargling could have been attributed to the desperation of a drowning man. At least, it was the kind of noise Lavinia imagined a drowning man might make.

She contemplated these things while enjoying a quiet morning soak in the bath. There was nothing calling, apart from the bedding that had to be ironed, but that could wait. The sun streamed through the bathroom window. It would be a good day to go to the garden centre and choose some roses, she thought, and I could treat myself to lunch, or at the very least have one of Luigi's excellent cappuccinos in the café.

Lavinia pushed aside the remnants of her breakfast and opened the rose catalogue. She'd made a fresh cafetière and Dermot O'Leary was just about to play Jack Savoretti's latest single on the radio when the back door opened and Fergus appeared. He looked a bit rough. He hadn't shaved and didn't appear to have combed his hair.

'Why on earth are you back so soon?' she said. 'Has something happened? Why didn't you call me?'

Fergus slumped into a chair by the table.

'Well, I didn't want to disturb you. It was early when I set off and then... well, I just kept going really. The thing is, I took a bit of a tumble last night and didn't sleep much. Didn't feel too good this morning, not up to mauling with sheep at any rate. So I thought I'd best come home.'

By the time he had managed to get his coat off, Lavinia had already made him a cup of strong sweet tea. 'Just get this down you,' she said. 'And tell me what crazy thing you were doing to upend yourself.'

'I wasn't doing anything crazy actually,' retorted Fergus. 'It was a simple error of judgement. They've got wooden floors in a split-level room. I thought there were two steps but there were three. It's these damned bifocals. They play tricks you know.'

'Well, that's as maybe,' said Lavinia, 'but it's just as likely you weren't watching where you were putting your feet. Did you do any damage? You're no featherweight to go throwing yourself around people's sitting rooms.'

'Only to myself' Fergus replied gloomily. 'I caught the side of my chest on a small table. It hurts a bit. Have we got any of those things you take for your back? I could do with some I think.'

'Yes, but get your shirt up and let me see what's what first.'

Lavinia could tell he was in pain just untucking his shirt from his trousers, and he had a sizeable bruise on the right side of his chest. He winced when she touched it. Drawing on distant memories of a single evening's first aid lecture at the W.I., she instructed him to take a deep breath.

'How was that?'

'Oh, I can breathe okay, but it hurts like hell.'

'You've probably cracked a rib,' she said. 'You should go to A&E to check it out.'

'Oh, don't fuss,' said Fergus. 'Just give me a couple of those pills and I'll go and lie down for a bit. I'll be fine when I catch up on some sleep. No need to go bothering doctors.'

'You would be bothering a mechanic without batting an eyelid if there was something wrong with the car. Doctors do get paid for being bothered you know and I'm sure they'd rather assess any damage now than deal with a punctured lung later.'

'It's only a bruise, Lavinia. You've been watching too many accident and emergency programmes. Just get me those pills will you?'

Now irritated beyond measure, he was struggling to get to his feet and prevent his unfastened trousers from falling down.

'When did you last eat?' quizzed Lavinia.

'What? What's that got to do with anything?'

'You're not supposed to take Ibuprofen on an empty stomach. I'll make you a couple of slices of toast.'

Fergus sat down with a groan, muttering under his breath, but Lavinia ignored him. She was not inclined to risk upsetting his fragile gastric equilibrium, even if he was.

On Sunday morning they spent three hours in A&E. Fergus had spent a bad night unable to get comfortable and Lavinia had laid the law down. Fergus was crotchety and impatient, alternating between brooding silences and critical outbursts.

'Keep your voice down,' hissed Lavinia. 'They are doing their best.'

Eventually he was called for X-ray and taken in to see a little American doctor who looked young enough to have been his granddaughter.

'I guess this must be pretty painful huh?' she said, studying the film of Fergus' chest.

Fergus beamed his megawatt beam at her.

'No, not too bad really doctor, but my wife insisted I come and check it out.'

Lavinia raised her eyebrows and shook her head.

'Good for her,' the doctor beamed back at him. 'There is a break, right here. Do you see? Fortunately, your lung is okay. Nothing to be done. We don't strap up chests any more but you do need to take it easy for a month or so while it heals. No strenuous upper body work. We don't want to see you back here as an emergency. I'll give you some strong painkillers to take for the first week or so and you take care when you are out and about, okay? I expect your good lady will keep an eye on you huh?'

Too right I will, thought Lavinia, as Fergus gushed his thanks and shook the doctor's hand.

The analgesics knocked Fergus out and he slept in his chair for the remainder of the day as Lavinia tiptoed around him. Later, as she ironed the sheets, which were now too dry, she reflected on how the weekend break she'd planned had evolved into something altogether different.

CHAPTER 11

A Question of Pockets

※

'I've got a hole in my leg,' Fergus announced in the middle of *Antiques Road Show*. Lavinia looked up from her RHS Rose Guide.

'What did you say?'

'Well, it's not my actual leg. It's in my trousers.'

'Oh, that's been there for ages. I assumed you were ignoring it.' Lavinia returned her attention to her book and several minutes passed while Fergus concentrated on an ancient firearm that had been unearthed from a cellar.

'Too far gone,' he pronounced. 'She's up a gum tree with that. Only fit for scrap I reckon. It really makes you wonder why they bother.' He turned to Lavinia. 'Could you get me a new pair next time you're out?'

'No.'

'Any particular reason? I thought you liked shopping.'

'The last time I bought trousers, if you can remember that far back, you said they didn't fit properly and they had inadequate pockets.'

'Yes they did. They were *standing-up* trousers, wouldn't hold anything except a few coins and they would fall out if one sat down.'

'I wasn't aware you'd even put them to the test. I'm fairly sure the price tag was still on when I took them to the charity shop. That's when I told you to buy your own trousers in future.'

Fergus' mouth set in a line and he returned his attention to the TV.

'Not more Beatles signatures!' he groaned. 'This used to be an antiques programme. It is fast becoming a Fiona Bruce memorabilia bonanza. We'll have another collection of Bolton Wanderers match tickets next. Can't remember the last time I saw Queen Anne legs or a half-decent portrait.'

'Why don't you turn it off then? It's obviously not doing your blood pressure any good.'

Fergus shot an offended glance in Lavinia's direction, but she was deep into David Austin's rose catalogue. He flicked through the channels until he found something about the *Mayflower* pilgrims and Lavinia reached for her noise-cancelling earphones.

Moments later she became aware of Fergus gesticulating wildly to attract her attention. At the very least she thought the Queen might have died.

'Where will I get trousers?' he demanded.

Lavinia sighed and put down her catalogue. There would be no peace until Fergus had got this bee out of his bonnet.

'I'm assuming you don't want to revisit Country Clobber.'

Fergus rolled his eyes, recalling the shock experienced by his wallet when he had bought a pair of winter cords from the aforementioned outfitter.

'In that case, your best bet is probably Marks & Spencer. I think they still cater for the older man with short legs and pocket issues.'

'Are you in there much these days?' tried Fergus.

'No, and I'm not buying your trousers for you Fergus.'

'Fine,' he said as he despatched the pilgrims in favour of *Landscape Artist of the Year*. Fergus was between a rock and a hard place. The health of his wallet was pitted against his abhorrence of the shopping centre. Lavinia turned her thoughts back to roses and left him to work it out. The holey trousers had been laundered twice more before he came up with a solution.

They had finished the shopping and Fergus was pulling

out of the supermarket car park when he put his plan into action.

'Would you mind if we popped into the shopping centre while we're out this way? Only I ordered a book and I need to collect it. You could nip into M & S for your extra bits and we could meet up for a coffee if you like.'

Lavinia suppressed a smile. For a man who hadn't a clue about subterfuge, he'd succeeded in getting her exactly where he wanted her. She let him continue thinking he was winning and contented herself with, 'That's fine. Did you forget we have a local bookshop?'

'Er, yes,' mumbled Fergus. 'I guess I did.'

The café was crowded with midday snackers. As there was no sign of Fergus, Lavinia bought a large cappuccino and made for the last table for two. She'd almost finished her coffee by the time he appeared with a huge carrier bag. It crossed Lavinia's mind that he might have already bought some trousers, but then she noticed the logo on the bag.

'That's a very large carrier for a book.'

'Yes. Sorry, have you been waiting long? I was passing The Works, so I nipped in for a couple of canvases and a sketch pad.'

'Making hay while the sun shines?' suggested Lavinia.

'Mm, something like that.' Fergus grinned. 'Another coffee?'

'Yes please, and a scone.' She felt she needed sustenance if she were to keep her cool during the next phase of Fergus' agenda.

The wallet didn't approve of cappuccino, so it bought two regular black with cold milk and a small fruitless scone with one pack of butter. As Fergus plonked the tray down he cut to the chase.

'Perhaps we could have a quick look at trousers on the way back to the car.'

Lavinia poured the tiniest drop of milk into her coffee and buttered her scone.

'We? Do you recall what I said concerning trousers?'

'Of course, but I do value your opinion you know.'

'Fergus, that's rubbish. When have you ever paid any attention to what I think about clothes? You have always been a law unto yourself. You just want to avoid the hassle of sorting through and looking at labels. That's what this whole palaver has been about. Be honest.'

Fergus did have the grace to look sheepish over the rim of his cup.

'Have I been rumbled?'

'Of course, you've been rumbled you old fool. We've lived together a long time. Remember?'

The men's' department had been given a make-over in

line with modern shopping trends. The display staff had mixed shirts, trousers, sweaters and jackets in colour coordinated blocks, which made no sense to Fergus as he wandered amongst them.

'It's a bloody nightmare in here. You can't see the wood for the trees. Why the hell don't they put all the trousers in one place?'

'Because, these days, many men like to buy a complete outfit and they want to see all the items together.'

'Men don't do that stuff,' grizzled Fergus. 'When they need a pair of trousers, they want to go in, buy them and get the hell out.'

Lavinia's patience was wearing thin.

'That's you. It's not all men.'

'It's all the men I know.'

'So, when was the last time you had a conversation about buying trousers with one of your acquaintances, or anybody other than me?'

Fergus changed the subject. 'Look at the legs! Why are they all so narrow? I couldn't move in those, let alone put anything in the pockets. There must be some proper trousers in here surely.'

Lavinia sighed. 'Why don't you just bite the bullet and go back to Country Clobber? Plenty of wide legs in there.'

The wallet squirmed in its jacket pocket and Fergus refocused on the task in hand. He homed in on a bargain rail of straight legs that would do at a pinch and selected a dark blue pair with a thirty-four-inch waist.

'Are you sure you're a thirty-four?' queried Lavinia.

'Always have been.'

'Be good to try them on though, to check the fit – and the pockets.'

Fergus didn't want to try them on. He'd had enough.

'Don't expect me to return them if they're not right and bear in mind they are on a 'reduced' rail, so they'll sell quickly,' Lavinia warned him. Fergus huffed and puffed as she pointed him in the direction of the fitting rooms.

He returned fairly speedily. 'Too small,' he snapped. 'I'll have to get a thirty-six. They must have changed the sizing.'

The choice of colour in the larger size boiled down to black, black or red. Lavinia suddenly felt weary. Fergus had a thing about black. He called it a non-colour, wouldn't even wear black shoes. Lavinia would have liked to sit down, as the very real prospect of Fergus plummeting into a dark mood loomed.

In fact, to her astonishment. he did the complete opposite and suddenly cheered up.

'I'll have the red ones. That's a great colour.'

'You can't wear red at your age. You'll look ridiculous.'

'I don't see why,' said Fergus 'Jonny Ringo' McFadden

wears red trousers in his YouTube videos. He looks pretty good in them and he's not that much younger than me.'

'But you've never worn anything red,' protested Lavinia.

'I'll have you know old thing, in my youth, I had a pair of suede desert boots with red laces. They would have looked stunning with these trousers. I quite fancy another pair.' Observing Lavinia's expression, he added, 'Not today of course. You look about done in.'

Lavinia trailed behind him to the pay point.

'Did you check the pockets?' she asked.

'No, I completely forgot, but I'm sure they'll be fine.'

CHAPTER 12

Out of the Comfort Zone

※

Lavinia thumped her bag on the kitchen table and sat down with her head in her hands. She needed to think, but almost immediately Fergus came bumbling in from the garden.

'You okay old thing? Shall I make the coffee? You look as though you could do with one.'

Lavinia raised her head. 'The nurse said my blood sugar level is up.'

'That's not the end of the world is it?' said Fergus. 'Can't you just take an extra pill or a higher dose or something?'

'Blood sugar, not blood pressure. Blood sugar is a whole new ball game. It goes with diabetes.'

'Oh, I see, bit of a bugger then,' he said handing her the biscuit tin. 'Here, have one of these lovely chocolate cookies. It will cheer you up.'

Lavinia glared at him in disbelief.

'What?' he retorted, and then the penny dropped. 'No more chocolate cookies eh?'

Lavinia shook her head.

'Jeeez!' said Fergus. He took a huge bite of his biscuit and picked up another as he sat down beside her. Lavinia snapped the lid on the tin and moved it to the other side of the table.

'So, what's the plan then?' he asked.

'There is no plan except the obvious, cut out the sugar, cut out the alcohol and chocolate and take more exercise – get a dog perhaps.'

'Wey hey! Stop there old thing. We agreed right at the beginning, remember? No kids, no four-legged things or feathers.'

'Circumstances change, Fergus.'

'Agreed, but some things are non-negotiable and that is one of them.'

'If I'd had the foresight, which regrettably I did not, I would have added drums to that list,' snapped Lavinia. She drained her mug, put it in the dishwasher and went out into the garden, calling back at him, 'thank you for your sympathy and support.'

Lavinia rarely gave way to emotions, but her eyes

were misty as she snipped at the dead heads on her roses. Frustration and anger bubbled to the surface. Her body had let her down. It was damned unfair after she'd made a concerted effort to eat good food and a balanced diet. She accepted that chocolate and red wine were her weakness, but when Fergus was at his obstreperous best, nothing else worked, short of throwing something. She would have to find another strategy. Take up yoga or become a Buddhist. She shuddered at the prospect.

Lavinia shared her dilemma with Helen, her closest friend, at their next moanathon get together. Over a couple of Americanos (cappuccino now being off limits), Helen put her mind to Lavinia's situation.

'Have you thought of joining a gym darling?'

'At my age? Pffff! Besides, you know I hate getting hot and sweaty.'

'Good for stress busting though, and it burns off a lot of calories. There are a lot of oldies in there strutting their stuff. I mean older than us.'

Lavinia sighed. 'I'm not sure I've got any stuff left to strut.'

'Rubbish, sweetie,' said Helen. 'You'd be surprised. Come and see. We'll have a coffee, and you can just get the feel of it. No hot and sweaty, I promise.'

Things did not bode well from the outset. Lavinia was

discomfited by not knowing what to wear. Helen's gym was run in tandem with a country club on the outskirts of town, very upmarket and very expensive. In a panic she rang her friend.

'Don't fret about it sweetie,' said Helen. 'Something really casual will be fine. You know, comfy, stretchy, a fleece; honestly, anything goes.'

Not a single item in Lavinia's wardrobe could be classified as either stretchy or fleecy. Finally, she selected a cream polo shirt, a pair of navy pull-on jersey trews and a blue zippered jacket she'd bought in desperation on a freezing cold day the previous June and forgotten to send to the charity shop. She slipped her feet into a pair of flats and grabbed her handbag. Fortunately she caught sight of herself in the hall mirror on the way out and realised the handbag looked ridiculous.

'Why are you doing this to yourself?' she asked the mirror. She stuffed her purse, keys and a packet of tissues into a small black canvas shoulder bag she kept in the cupboard under the stairs. It was quite the wrong colour, but she was in uncharted waters anyway and past caring.

The gym was never going to be Lavinia's 'go to' place for chilling out or revving up. A noxious potpourri of Dove and Lynx wafted just above that of bodies and socks and made her nauseous. The pool belched out chlorine every time someone opened the door. The music was loud and insistent. Machines whirred and clicked as fluorescent Lycra-clad riders, rowers and lifters pitted themselves relentlessly against their previous best.

'Of course, this is the crème de la crème,' Helen reassured her as they sat in the gallery with their coffee. 'There are sessions for beginners. I could book you in as a guest if you like.'

But Lavinia had already decided against exposing all her flabby bits to the world at large. This environment was too raw and altogether too bouncy for her.

The crux of the matter was that she saw no point in exercise for its own sake. Her days were busy in the house and garden. She used stairs instead of escalators, parked and walked when she could and did most of her own decorating because Fergus was so slap happy with anything other than a pointed squirrel hairbrush by Winsor and Newton. So she did not class herself among the... what did they call them now, sofa potatoes? Something like that anyway.

The prospect of diabetes appalled her, and the nurse had left her in no doubt that her card was marked if she failed to adjust her diet and increase her fitness level. It was useless talking to Fergus about it. The best thing he could come up with was, 'You could try running up and down the stairs a few times a day, old thing.' To which she'd replied, 'Knees, Fergus.'

'Mmm,' he said, from behind *The Times Culture Supplement*. 'I know what you mean. Bit of a bugger this old age stuff. Thank God for power tools and chocolate biscuits.'

The cushion flattened the paper on to Fergus's face as Lavinia stormed out.

Chance played a significant part in determining her next course of action. She was heading towards the community centre to enquire about Tai Chi classes and stopped off at the Post Office, where a poster caught her eye:

'Get Fit, Stay Fit In Later Life.' A talk for senior citizens. Guidelines towards Health and Independence.
No mats, no machines, no special clothes.

Lavinia noted the details and put the Tai Chi on hold.

As it turned out, she learned little more than she already knew. But the speaker, a bouncy woman in stretchy trousers and a hooded jumper, did go on at length about the benefits of drinking lots of water and brisk walking, which was Lavinia's *bête noir*. Walking with a capital W made her back ache and played havoc with her knees. She raised this point during questions at the end, to a chorus of empathetic 'me toos' from the audience.

Bouncy lady laughed. 'I was expecting that one but actually, all you need is a decent pair of trainers.'

It was the audience's turn to laugh and there was much muttering along the lines of water tablets, laughing stocks, not a good look with tweed and hanging out with Ed Sheeran next.

Undeterred, Miss Bouncy continued to wax lyrical about quality trainers. 'They cost more,' she told them, 'because they are scientifically constructed to cushion your feet and support your joints. I promise you, a good pair will change the way you feel about walking.'

Lavinia didn't buy Miss Bouncy's spiel and thought the whole set up was sponsored by the manufacturers to part pensioners from their pennies. Despite her cynicism however, on one of her shopping jaunts, she paused outside the sports shop window to consider the display of shoes. They were, without exception, the ugliest things. She was about to walk on when it struck her that orthopaedic shoes were also aesthetically grim. Perhaps there was a connection. Purely in the interests of consumer research, she decided to investigate.

The huge plate glass doors closed behind her with a soft swish and the sensation of being swallowed by a monstrous alien creature was overwhelming. Metal crates, stacked either side of her, spewed out white T-shirts, white socks, white shorts like the aftermath of an orthodontic catastrophe. Drooping sports bags clung to chrome structures like withering fruits clinging to an alien tree. Further in, floor to ceiling displays of single trainers mesmerised her. Boxes stacked like giant Rubik's Cubes created a wall through the centre of the store. The relentless beat of the music wiped Lavinia's brain. To hell with consumer research, she thought. This was a very bad idea.

At that moment a skinny young man appeared from behind a bag tree; haircut like a hedgehog, jogging bottoms at half mast, tucked into boots he'd forgotten to lace up. The huge badge on his sweatshirt read: 'DECATHLON SPORT/JEZ /HERE TO HELP'.

'Do you need any help?'

Get me out of here, was the first thing that came to Lavinia's mind. The second was that if anyone needed help it was Jez, just getting himself dressed for a start, but what actually came out was, 'Well, I came in to look at trainers, but it appears to be more complicated than I imagined so I think perhaps I'll leave it thank you.'

Jez had been well coached. 'Were you looking for yourself madam?'

'That was the idea yes.'

'And what were you planning to use the trainers for?'

'What kind of question is that?' Lavinia asked. 'Generally, when I buy shoes I walk about a bit in them like most people.'

Unfazed by her retort, Jez explained there were different styles for different activities, tennis or running, aerobics or basketball for instance.

Lavinia laughed. 'Do I look like a person who might do any of those things?' she said.

He smiled and shrugged. 'To be honest madam, you can never tell these days.'

Very diplomatic, thought Lavinia, and decided to engage with him.

'I need to do more walking,' she said. 'But my knees are a bit dodgy and it makes my back ache.'

'Good trainers may well help,' he told her. 'I could show you what we have if you like.'

Consumer research was back on the table. After looking at several examples, it seemed lamentable to Lavinia that in order to benefit from scientific advancement, it was necessary to wrap one's feet in glitzy pastel colours or fluorescent abominations.

'Jez,' she said, 'These trainers are fine for your generation but, when one is sixty-five plus, one looks for something a little more modest, less flashy.'

He produced a black pair with a single purple stripe.

'Now those are much more appropriate,' said Lavinia.

He loosened the laces, inserted some gel insoles, and handed them to her. 'Pop your feet into those,' he instructed, 'and tell me what you think.'

It crossed Lavinia's mind that this was extending the boundaries of her research, but she did slip off her shoes.

From that moment on, the trainers hardly left her feet.

'They're amazing,' she told Fergus. 'It's like walking on a cloud.'

'Not very pretty though,' he replied. 'Especially with that skirt, old thing.'

Lavinia didn't reply. She was already planning her next research project into modest, stretchy trousers.

CHAPTER 13

Enter Charlie, Stage Left

There could be no doubt that if cats had a kingdom, Charlie would be king. He oozed essence of big cat from every filament of his tiger-striped tabby coat, his magnificent leonine whiskers a testament to his feline prowess. To compensate for the vet's unspeakable savagery, he had developed attitude and honed his hunting skills to degree level. Even half-grown rabbits had to be on red alert when Charlie was on the prowl. Any humankind encountered during his daily patrols of the gardens in his patch were met with practised disdain, condescending affection being reserved for the farmer's widow who had been persuaded, against her better judgment, that he would be company for her. But Charlie would be no one's lap cat and no amount of doting on her part made the slightest impression.

Charlie monitored the activity on Lavinia's bird table with the intensity of a sniper, much to Lavinia's annoyance. If their paths crossed, he arched his back, rising to his full height and locked eyes with her in an icy green glare before streaking off under the fence into the paddock to top up his breakfast.

'If that bloody cat has my wren or the robin, I'll boil him in oil,' she told Fergus. 'Why doesn't he sit under his own bird table?'

'Probably because the old girl can't get out there any more to put anything on it,' Fergus replied. 'I could do with him spending the night in the studio if I could catch him. I've got a family of mice in there he could have with pleasure. But then he'd probably crap in there as well, so I'll stick to my traps.'

'You'd never catch him anyway. He's like greased lightning.'

On the day that the old lady had a fall and the ambulance whisked her off to hospital, Charlie went AWOL.

'What about the cat?' the neighbours asked.

'Scarpered probably,' said one.

'He'll be back when the dust settles,' said another.

'We'll leave some dried food and water outside,' said

the relatives. 'Mum will be back in a couple of days. He's an old cat but he'll be fine.'

The old lady didn't come back, and neither did Charlie. Nor did the relatives come with any more food. A couple of weeks went by before Charlie was sighted down the lane by a neighbour who put some cat biscuits and water by the old lady's door. Something ate them, so she refilled the dishes each day. After another week Charlie appeared when she arrived with more food. Now a shadow of his former self, he was nervous and diffident.

Then word came that the old lady was not coming back at all. She was going to live with her daughter.

'So what about the cat?'

'Oh, they don't want the cat, but the grandson is moving into the house.'

There was much tutting over garden fences.

For weeks, Charlie wafted round the neighbourhood like a wraith, reacting like a wild creature on sight of humans. As soon as the old lady's grandson moved into the house everyone took their eyes off Charlie. He was out of sight and out of mind.

That is, until the day Lavinia spotted him curled up under a bush close to her bird table. The birds were going about their business without a care in the world. She looked at the cat carefully. Perhaps it wasn't Charlie at all. Its coat was a dull coarse grey. Its mournful eyes looked back at her, but it made no attempt to move.

'There's a tabby cat in the garden,' she remarked to Fergus. 'I thought it was Charlie, but I don't think it can be. It's just sitting there.'

Fergus was washing all his palettes in the Belfast sink again.

'I do wish you'd do that in the utility room,' she snapped.

'Light's better in here old thing. Stop fretting. I'll clean up. Then I'll go and look at your cat if it's still there.'

'It's not my cat! We don't do cats or dogs, as you forcefully reminded me not so long ago.'

Fergus' vehement reaction to her suggestion that it might be nice to have a dog to walk with still burned. She couldn't bear to watch the multi-coloured disaster happening in her sink, so she went to clean the bathroom instead.

Fergus' voice bellowed up the stairs, penetrating the noise of the Hoover. She switched it off. 'Is there a problem?'

'I said, have we got any tinned tuna?'

'Why?' said Lavinia looking at her watch. It was only eleven-thirty, not even close to lunchtime.

'Have we got any?' shouted Fergus.

'Of course we have. It's in the cupboard. Only it's not in a tin. It's in a jar. Why do you need to know?'

Lavinia stood at the top of the stairs looking down at him, trying to figure out the expression on his face.

'Charlie is at the back door. He looks terrible. I've given him some milk but he's still mewing at me. I think he's starving.'

Lavinia opened her mouth, but no words came out. For once she was speechless. By the time she reached the kitchen Fergus had already opened a three-pound fifty-nine pence jar of line-caught albacore tuna and was spooning it into a Royal Doulton pudding bowl.

'You are not giving that to a cat!' she roared at him.

He stopped mid-spoon and just looked at her before saying quietly, 'Well, what else have you got that a cat can eat?'

'You shouldn't be giving him anything. He doesn't belong to us. If you feed him once he'll keep coming back.'

'Just go and look at him Lavinia, and then tell me whether or not I should give him some of your precious tuna. Because I'm damn sure no-one else has fed him for quite a while. And he's too weak to catch anything for himself.'

'Just for the record, how did you suddenly become an expert in cat physiology after forty years as a signed-up member of the 'Ban Fur and Four Legs' Brigade?' Lavinia was steaming. 'Charlie isn't even an amiable creature.'

Fergus sighed. 'I always had a cat when I was a kid,' he said. 'But the last one was special. She was a phenomenal hunter, even brought home a pheasant once.

She got caught in a trap and was missing for days. After we found her I nursed her back to full health. Then the gamekeeper poisoned her. I vowed there and then never to keep another animal. But I can't stand by and see one suffer.' Fergus sniffed and blew his nose. 'Have you got another dish instead of this posh thing? I wasn't thinking.'

Without a word Lavinia, handed him a small baking dish and watched him break up the fish into small pieces with a fork.

Charlie fell on the dish and cleared it in seconds, licking every last scrap from each corner. He inspected the empty milk saucer and looked up at Fergus expectantly. Lavinia handed him the jar of tuna.

'You'd better give him the rest of it. I'll get him some more milk.'

During the course of that day, every time they opened the back door Charlie appeared, tail held high, miaowing at full volume. He put away another tin of tuna Lavinia found at the back of the cupboard, a tin of sardines and almost a pint of milk.

The following morning, when Fergus stepped outside to check the temperature, Charlie was sunning himself on the patio. He immediately rose to rub himself round Fergus's legs.

'He's back. Have we got anything for him?' he called to Lavinia.

'I'm not surprised he's back, considering the gourmet fare on offer yesterday. There's one tin of pilchards. They're in tomato sauce but I suppose you could rinse them under the tap. After that, unless he likes sweetcorn and assorted pulses, you will have to go and buy some cat food.'

Charlie coped just as well with the pilchards and the sauce, polishing off a whole tin in two sittings, along with a third of a pint of milk.

'You are aware you're making a rod for your own back with this aren't you?' Lavinia asked Fergus. 'Now that you've unleashed your inner cat rescuer, you are committed. Old furry four-legs could be here for a while.'

'Oh, an outside cat is fine,' he said. 'They do their own thing.'

Lavinia recalled how Charlie used to spend his days curled up on the old lady's pink candlewick bedspread and wondered if Charlie remembered. No doubt they would find out when the weather turned cooler.

CHAPTER 14

Old Peculier

In their youth Lavinia and Fergus had enjoyed several trips into France, all organised by Lavinia. She took charge of passports, tickets, currency, and logistics while Fergus and his camera trundled along marvelling at the stained glass, the carvings, the standing stones, the basketry, and the museums. Lavinia engaged her A level French and bought tickets, found places to stay and things to eat. Fergus eventually mastered the single French phrase, '*Un cognac s'il vous plait monsieur,*' simply because Lavinia refused to go to the bar and order for him. When they were able to afford a car it was Lavinia who drove, having passed her test at nineteen. Fergus, after his second failure, assumed the role of navigator in chief and observer of things of special interest in the countryside.

This became the default setting for all future holidays and endured even when Fergus finally got his licence. He was, to be fair, a hot shot with a map, which Lavinia was not, and she regarded Fergus' driving style as somewhat erratic, to put it mildly. It was an arrangement that worked particularly well for Fergus. He enjoyed being a passenger.

Not long after he retired, Fergus had made an executive decision that henceforth he, that is they, would holiday in the UK. He had also declared his preferred destination to be the south coast of Pembrokeshire.

'Why Pembrokeshire over and above the rest of the British Isles?' queried Lavinia.

'It's peaceful,' said Fergus.

'And?'

'It's an easy drive.'

'So are the Lleyn Peninsula and Aberdyfi. Why Pembrokeshire?'

'Well, it's not particularly popular,' Fergus mumbled.

'And?' Lavinia persisted.

'What do you want me to say?'

'I want you to convince me that Pembrokeshire should take precedence as our holiday destination for the foreseeable future.'

'Don't you like it?'

'Yes! But that's not the point.'

'Well, you'd have to agree that the beaches and the coastal paths are stunning and from my perspective... as an artist I mean...'

'Fergus, you are still evading my question.'

Fergus removed his glasses and, selecting the only corner of his handkerchief that hadn't wiped a paint brush, began to polish them. Lavinia waited while he checked the lenses by squinting through them at the light and polished some more. Finally he connected with her.

'I'm sorry Lavinia, but I can't do motorway stuff any more. It's just too stressful. I get so anxious that I can't live in my skin.'

'Okay, I'll buy that, but you still haven't explained Pembrokeshire.'

'It's happy memories, I think. I used to go a lot when I was a kid. My grandparents had a place near Solva – port in a storm, you could say.'

Lavinia was quiet. Fergus had never said much about his early life and she had never asked.

'Are we in a storm, Fergus?' she ventured.

'No, of course not old thing. I just have a yen to go back. I don't know how to explain but it's something about being rather than doing. Do you know what I mean?'

Lavinia wasn't sure that she did. But for the sake of Fergus' peace of mind, which inevitably impacted on her own, she was prepared to go along with it. Besides, like many other notions that had taken his fancy over the years, she assumed it would eventually fall away.

Ten years on, the little place she had found had become an established factor in their lives. For one week in June they returned, like swallows to the old nest, rejoicing in its familiarity and revisiting best loved places. The cottage was ideally situated with a breathtaking view over Saint Bride's bay. It was comfortable, bright and well equipped without being cluttered. Fergus was happy and there was little for him to grumble about apart from his annual rant.

'Those bloody seagulls were jumping on the roof and screeching at four-thirty again this morning!'

Lavinia's response, every year, was a variation on a theme.

'It's the seaside, Fergus. Gulls do what gulls do. You'll just have to sleep with your deaf ear uppermost or stick your fingers in.'

Fergus grunted, as was his wont, and didn't mention it again. To Lavinia's surprise she found she enjoyed the holiday almost as much as Fergus, and as soon as they arrived home she made a diary note to rebook early.

Fergus watched Lavinia struggling to fit the box of Christmas decorations back into the cupboard under the stairs.

'I'd offer to help,' he said, 'but you seem to have a system going there.'

'Thank you very much,' she replied from the depths. 'but it is your devil-may-care method of hurling things in that is the fundamental problem in here, that along with you standing in the exact spot that blocks the light.'

Fergus chortled. 'Okay, I'll put the kettle on and make some coffee for when you return to the surface.'

Lavinia appeared in the kitchen looking ruffled. Grabbing a handful of tissues, she wiped her face and neck and stretched her back with a groan.

'I'm getting too old for scrabbling about in small spaces,' she announced as she collapsed on to a chair.

Fergus handed her a mug of coffee and a flapjack. She glared at him. 'You know I don't do sugar.'

'Extenuating circumstances,' he replied. 'You're stressed. Eat half. It's not going to kill you.'

'That is not exactly helpful. I'm trying to re-educate my palate away from sweet things.'

Fergus bit into his second sticky biscuit. 'By the way,' he mumbled through the crumbs, 'what date are we going away this year?'

Lavinia's mug came to a halt halfway to her mouth. She closed her eyes and let out a long breath before she replied.

'I forgot,' she said quietly.

'Well, we can look it up, can't we?'

'I don't mean I forgot the date. I completely forgot to book it and you didn't remind me.'

'I don't do reminding,' said Fergus. 'That's your job.'

'Oh, for goodness sake, it's not about jobs. It completely slipped my mind with all the fuss around Christmas going on.'

Lavinia absently picked up her flapjack and took a large bite. Fergus noticed but said nothing.

'I'll do it today,' she said.

She drained her mug, crammed the remains of the biscuit into her mouth and stood up, unaware that she had just broken her own cardinal rule.

'I can't believe you let me forget!' she called, on her way to the study. Fergus didn't reply. He was contemplating whether or not a third flapjack would wreck his appetite for lunch.

Lavinia was unusually quiet as they ate their cheese on toast.

'You seem very far away,' Fergus ventured. 'Are you okay?'

'Yes, I'm fine.'

'Did you manage to sort out the holiday?'

'No, not yet.'

'Oh, I thought you said you were going to book it this morning.'

'I did and I was. It appears that our cottage is fully

booked from May bank holiday until the middle of September.'

Fergus took a moment or two to absorb this information.

'There must be other places that are still available though. It is only January for God's sake.'

'Yes of course there are, hundreds! But very few that match the Fergus Moreton specifications.'

'Lavinia, I'm not that hard to please. If it's quiet, comfy, not too far from a decent restaurant and the beach, I'm a happy man.'

Lavinia raised her eyebrows.

'Perhaps you'd like to sit by the computer with me then, while I trawl through all the possibles?'

'Good Lord no! Can't think of anything worse. I'm sure you'll find something that fits the bill, old thing. You're very good at that stuff and, actually, there's something I want to try out in the studio this afternoon.'

He stood up, scraping the chair legs across the tile floor. Lavinia winced and waved her hand in dismissal. He blew her a kiss and shot off like a small boy let off the hook.

Within an hour of arrival at their holiday destination, Lavinia was musing on how she had managed to select a cottage that was so patently unsuitable. She had known before they'd even arrived.

Fergus let rip as she negotiated an uphill hairpin turn into a narrow lane.

'What the hell? I thought you said this place was accessible. God forbid that we meet something coming the other way. It's a bloody nightmare.'

Lavinia, who was approaching the end of her driving tether, retorted, 'On the website it said, 'Approached via a country lane.' It did not say a single track with grass down the middle and giant nettles that thrust themselves through the windows to sting your neck, obviously, or I wouldn't have booked it.'

It soon became apparent that the approach was not the only area in which the letting company had been economical with the truth. The 'ample parking space' was a meagre pull-in, at an awkward angle, that required the skills of a forklift truck driver. As Lavinia finally succeeded in getting their small Fiat out of harm's way, Fergus quipped, 'Bloody good job we didn't come in the Land Cruiser!'

Lavinia was not in the mood for wry humour. She concentrated instead on finding the key under the pot in the 'charming country garden'. Said garden was laid out on a descending slope below road level. Dominated by several huge trees and two ponds, 'netted for safety', any charm there might have been was offset by treacherous steps and walkways without handrails.

'Nice little drop of rain and this lot could be a death trap, I reckon,' said Fergus.

Lavinia's spirits were falling, like mercury before a storm, in direct correlation with her rising blood pressure. She willed herself to stay calm, but as she opened the door of the cottage her heart sank. The interior decor appeared to have been inspired by a beef stew with side orders of butternut squash and sweet potato. Every windowsill, shelf and flat surface strained under the weight of brass, copper, china, candles, pebbles and shells. Every wall was hung with clocks, mirrors, and pictures, all displayed with the random artistic verve of a child let loose with a hammer and a few nails.

Fergus, whose life had revolved around art and design, stood in the doorway holding two bags of holiday essentials and surveyed the scene. Lavinia held her breath.

'Jeez,' he said. 'Time for a beer I think.'

Setting down the bags, he dug out a bottle of Old Peculier, flipped the top off with his pocketknife and drank half out of the bottle. Lavinia found a glass and decanted the remainder into it as Fergus kicked off his shoes and stretched out on the sofa with his eyes closed. Lavinia located her teabags and in the brownest of brown kitchens, made herself a pot of Earl Grey before flopping into an armchair. The clocks ticked around them. A solitary fly bumped against the window.

'Well, at least the bit about it being quiet was right,' she said.

'So far,' Fergus replied gloomily.

He took several gulps of his beer and fell back into the cushions, surveying the bric-à-brac on the shelves and walls.

'It's death by trinket in here,' he declared.

'Oh, for goodness sake Fergus, do you have to be so dismal? Okay, it's not what we're used to but the rest of Pembrokeshire is still out there to enjoy.'

'As long as you survive the treachery of that hellish track.'

Lavinia let him have the last word. There was no point in arguing when Fergus had dug himself into a hole. She closed her eyes and dozed off.

Almost an hour later she woke to sounds of frantic shuffling and grunting. It took her a few seconds to reorientate herself and to realise the kerfuffle was being created by Fergus. He was stranded on his back on the sofa like a distressed sheep in a hedge.

'I can't get out of this thing.' he growled. 'It is so bloody squashy I've sunk. Can you give me a hand?'

Once on his feet, he bumbled towards the open wooden staircase with its single handrail.

'Shoes, Fergus!' Lavinia yelled to stop him in his tracks.

'What?' he paused, one foot on the polished step.

'Put your shoes on. Those stairs are lethal in socks. You'll break your neck.'

Lavinia slept badly that night. She ruminated on how her judgement had completely failed her. She was going over and over the property description in her head trying to detect something she'd missed.

A colony of rooks in the trees outside the bedroom set up their rowdy parliamentary business just before four in the morning. Fergus got up, cursing, and slammed the windows.

That day Lavinia suggested they walk along the beach at Newgale. It had never failed to raise Fergus' spirits. They had Sunday lunch in one of their favourite pubs, but Fergus remained very switched off while Lavinia quietly tried to come to terms with having messed up their holiday and wondered how to rectify it. The lane, the parking, the sofa, the birds, and the trinkets all seemed to be gaining the upper hand. The following day they lunched in Solva before tackling a section of the coastal path. The sun was warm. A light breeze ruffled Lavinia's hair but Fergus didn't seem to engage with any of it. That evening, after a double fix of Old Peculier, he blurted out, 'This just isn't working is it? I'm so sorry, but this place just gets me down. I feel very bad about it because it's your holiday too, but... I'd really like to go home.'

Although Lavinia was not one for quitting, she knew that prolonging Fergus' stress and discomfiture would be counterproductive. There was so much she could have said. But it wouldn't change anything.

CHAPTER 15

No Cause for Alarm

Fergus would have no truck with technology. What's more, he had turned active avoidance of the trappings of the modern world into an art form, unless it happened to suit his purpose in the studio or the garden.

Lavinia had been astonished when he had splashed out on an iPad after a young niece had demonstrated its attributes for an artist. And then David Hockney, no less, had exhibited work he'd created also using an iPad. Fergus had been entertained by his new toy for a while but was beginning to lose interest when the same niece told him about YouTube. Here Fergus found videos of lumberjacks felling trees without chainsaws and tribesmen hacking canoes from tree trunks with axes.

Not to mention Jonny 'Ringo' McFadden's drumming tutorials. Instantly Fergus was in video heaven. He never sent emails or read any sent to him. Nor did he bother with software updates. Software was a complete mystery to Fergus, so he could see no good reason to update it.

Domestically, he was a disaster. He could manage the toaster and the hob, but the oven was an alien thing. The central heating controls were too complicated, and he refused to get his head round the washing machine, the dishwasher, replacement Hoover bags or the printer. In the aftermath of a power cut, when the phone insisted on being reset before it would resume normal function, it was Lavinia who sorted it out.

'What would you do if I dropped in a heap one day?' she asked him.

'I'd have to find a woman what does.'

'Well, good luck with that,' she chortled. 'You'll need to find one with the patience of a saint and skin like a rhinoceros.'

To be fair, Fergus did come into his own out of doors. He drew the line at roof tiles and chimney pots, but most other tasks were well within his remit. Drains, fences, trees, and blown-over things he coped with admirably.

'Well, you know where you are with a saw, a hammer and a few nails,' he was fond of saying. 'Can't be doing with all this wi-fi, gigabyte, bluetooth stuff. Life was much simpler when a thing was either on or it was off.'

Technological blips rapidly engaged Fergus' short fuse mode, which would send him into a fury like a toddler with a malfunctioning toy, so things did not bode well when an incessant beeping started up just as Lavinia was preparing to serve her specialty, fluffy omelette with new potatoes and spinach. Automatically, she checked the oven timer, although she hadn't used the oven. It was dormant.

'What's going on?' demanded Fergus, appearing in the kitchen like a pop-up character.

'Can you turn that thing off?'

'I would if I knew what it was but it's not in here,' Lavinia said.

'Where else would it be?' said Fergus. 'It isn't the smoke alarm. That lets out a deafening screech.'

'I know that. So, what the heck else is demanding attention just when I'm about to enjoy my dinner? Smoke alarm battery?'

'I don't think so. It doesn't sound like an urgent beep.'

'What about that thing up there? What's that?' said Fergus pointing to a small white box on the kitchen ceiling.

'You know what it is. It's a carbon monoxide sensor.'

'Really? Never noticed it before. When did we get that then? What kind of noise does it make?'

'Honestly, Fergus, I wonder if you actually inhabit

your own body sometimes. It was last year, and you *were* here at the time. I've no idea what it sounds like.'

'Have you left the phone off the hook?'

'I haven't used the phone today. Have you? And anyway, it doesn't beep, it whines. Fergus, why don't you just go on an investigative tour while I see if I can salvage our dinner? It's out there somewhere whatever it is. Although I'm beginning to feel as if it's inside my head.'

'I'll go and check the Sky box,' said Fergus. 'I wonder what that does when it's in distress?'

Lavinia put dinner on hold before following him into the sitting room. Fergus was on his knees with one ear to the Sky box, which was on a low shelf under the television.

'Nothing,' he said looking up sideways at her.

'Well, it is definitely louder in here,' she said. 'What the hell can it be? There is another carbon monoxide alarm near the wood burner, but it surely can't be that because the stove isn't lit.'

'Well I don't think there's a fire anywhere,' said Fergus. 'We'd be able to smell it by now.'

'Carbon monoxide is odourless,' offered Lavinia. 'That's why it's so dangerous.'

As Fergus struggled to get up off the floor, swearing

under his breath about the clapped-out state of his knees, he growled at Lavinia.

'I don't know about CO gas but that infernal noise is dangerous to my mental health. I can't hear myself think. Push that chair over, will you? I'll get up and have a look at that box. Do we know how to open it?'

He was already positioning a soft cushioned chair beneath the alarm when Lavinia interjected, 'For God's sake you'll break your bloody neck on that thing. Just hang on a minute while I get the steps from the shed.'

'I'll be all right. Don't fuss woman. The sooner we shut this thing up the better.' He clambered on to the chair by clinging on to the mantlepiece as Lavinia clung on to his belt, all the while thinking that if he fell, he would land on top of her, and that didn't bear thinking about.

'I can't see any way of opening this thing. It's a sealed unit.'

'It can't be sealed Fergus, because there's a battery inside.'

'Well I'm damned if I can find a way in. Do you want to try?'

'No, not really. Do you want me to ring the electrician and ask him?'

'Certainly not. He'll think we're a right pair of numpties.'

'He'd be spot on in this instance,' quipped Lavinia.

'I could ask Derek up the lane if you like. He knows everything about everything.'

'Yes, and the entire village will be having a giggle at our expense by tomorrow evening. No thanks, don't bother anyone. I'll take it off the ceiling. That'll shut it up and if it doesn't it can do its thing in the outside bin until the battery runs out. Bloody modern technological rubbish!'

Fergus clambered down off the chair and took the paint rag out of his pocket, wiping it across his damp forehead and leaving a red streak.

'I'll fetch the big screwdriver from the studio and yank it off.'

'If you're going to be yanking at things, bring the stepladder back with you. I'm not having you doing stuff like that standing on a squashy chair. That's just crazy.'

Fergus stomped off muttering about things doing his head in, and Lavinia returned to the kitchen, where it was marginally quieter. Her light and fluffy omelette had taken on the guise of a sodden wash leather. She tipped it in the bin and cracked four more eggs into a bowl. Fergus passed through the kitchen with the steps and an enormous screwdriver.

'This will sort it out,' he said as he disappeared towards the beeps. He was back a couple of minutes later with the offending alarm in his hands.

'Well, I've got it off, but I still can't see a way to shut it up,' he said.

Lavinia put her ear to the alarm, which was completely silent. The beeps were still going full pelt, but they were somewhere else.

'This is not the cause of the problem,' she said.

Fergus' face was a study. He put the box to his ear in disbelief.

'We looked. There isn't anything else in there. I think I must be going mad. It makes no sense.'

Lavinia walked into the lounge and looked round carefully. She returned to the kitchen holding a small travel clock that lived on a shelf just below the CO box. Its alarm was frantically beeping.

'You told me last night that the batteries were dead in this, which was why I didn't check it.'

'They were,' agreed Fergus. 'I put new ones in this afternoon.'

'Then I think you probably set the alarm at the same time Fergus.'

Lavinia switched it off. Fergus stared at the small timepiece, the red stripe across his forehead giving him the bewildered look of an American Indian confronted with a power tool.

'How come you didn't realise it was the clock then?' Fergus blustered.

'Oh, come on, we haven't used it for donkeys' years. I'd

forgotten what it sounds like and anyway, only yesterday you said it was dead,' Lavinia batted back.

'Bugger,' said Fergus looking down on the inert plastic box in his hand. 'Well I guess we need to know how to get into this contraption anyway. Perhaps you could ring the guy sometime and get him to explain before he puts it back.'

Lavinia picked up the omelette pan in a threatening manner and with the other hand hurled the wet dishcloth at Fergus' face with creditable accuracy.

CHAPTER 16

One False Move

Fergus was on a steep learning curve in his relationship with Charlie. From the outset, it was a battle of wills. Despite the fact that it took a couple of weeks for Charlie to establish his preferences, and for Fergus to accede to his demands, the cat appeared to have decided to stay.

When Fergus was in full cat rescue mode, Charlie's pitiful cries had prompted him to raid Lavinia's store cupboard and present the obviously starving cat with a dish of line-caught albacore tuna. He had followed this with sardines and pilchards from the same source. So, when Lavinia had insisted that he buy some Felix, that's what he bought. Charlie polished off two tins in no time flat.

'Jeez,' said Fergus. 'He's eaten one pound sixty pence in a day and a half.'

The wallet went into a spasm in response and Fergus implemented economies. After all, he reasoned, the creature was essentially a stray and Fergus thought he should be jolly grateful for having been rescued. However, Fergus' next purchase, of discount supermarket own brand cat food, was not at all well received. It was sniffed, sampled and ignored. Charlie had obviously decided he would rather survive on milk until something better turned up.

'He's started behaving like a typical picky cat,' Fergus complained as he scraped the shrivelled brown chunks into the bin.

Lavinia laughed. 'What did you expect? You've only yourself to blame. You started him off on the wrong foot.'

'Well, I certainly wasn't expecting to have to fork out for twenty-odd tins of prime kitty meat every month.'

'Oh, don't be an old skinflint. It's hardly going to cause a financial crisis is it? The poor thing is malnourished. He'll never recover on cheap stuff.'

'I seem to recall that you were the one that went off like a firecracker about me giving him tuna.'

'That was albacore tuna, Fergus. It's meant for discerning humans, not scraggy moggies, distressed or otherwise.'

The following day when Fergus forayed into the pet food aisle, he studied the alternatives to Felix and discovered Whiskas Beef on special offer. It was only pennies cheaper, but he was damned if he was going to be manipulated by a cat.

Charlie was unimpressed. He sniffed it and looked up at Fergus as if to say, 'You're not seriously expecting me to eat this?'

So Fergus shut the door and left him to it. Charlie ate a third and left the rest to go dry. Fergus put it in the fridge and added a fresh dollop on top before presenting it again. Charlie was not so easily fooled, and Lavinia went ballistic when she discovered a half-eaten cat dinner in her fridge.

'For a start, it has been on the floor and it's also had a cat's tongue all over it. The same tongue that licks its bum. Absolutely no! If he doesn't eat it, you'll have to throw it away. The answer is simple, Fergus. Buy fishy Felix.'

Round one went to Charlie. He liked Felix – a lot, especially the tuna variety.

While the days were warm and sunny, Charlie ate out on the patio, snoozed in the rose bed and appeared by his feeding station, on average, about five times a day. Most times he got lucky, but if Fergus was in full artistic flow, his felinophile instincts were on the back burner and he was heard to growl, 'Oh bugger off cat. You've been fed.'

Then the rain came, with a vengeance. Charlie turned up the first morning soaked and mewling. Lavinia took pity on him and put his dishes inside the porch door. Justifying it to Fergus with 'It was pelting down. He'd have had Felix soup in the space of two minutes. Besides, he was gone as soon as he'd finished.'

'I suppose he could be fed in the shed,' suggested Fergus.

'Yes, he could, and I could get soaked instead. But the shed is the obvious answer if you'd like to take on sole responsibility for feeding him. It's fine by me.'

Fergus grunted and disappeared into his studio.

The following morning Charlie nipped into the porch out of the rain as soon as the door was opened. Lavinia watched Fergus stroking his head before putting his breakfast down inside. This was obviously an arrangement that met with Charlie's approval, and before long he was performing his postprandial ablutions on the doormat with one eye on the outside world. His confidence grew. He ventured as far as the inside door just to check that food was about to be served and then one morning, unknown to Lavinia, he followed her into the utility room where she kept his supplies. It was a small room housing a sink unit, the washing machine and the secondary fridge freezer. The few visible floor tiles, which Fergus had refused to replace because most of them couldn't be seen, were a dismal shade of mottled brown. They blended well with Charlie's tabby markings, rendering him almost invisible from above. Not that Lavinia was looking down (why would she?) as she turned with his dish towards the porch and stood firmly on his tail. Pandemonium ensued as Charlie rounded on her leg, hissing and howling with claws fully extended. Felix chicken chunks in gravy spattered themselves over the fridge and the ironing pile as Lavinia struggled to regain her equilibrium.

'You stupid creature!' she yelled. 'What the hell were you doing under my feet?' Charlie shot through the open doors to the patio flicking his tail like a ringmaster's whip.

When Lavinia appeared to check if he was okay, he glared at her like the cat he had once been and hissed a warning before turning away and walking slowly towards the gate.

Lavinia, recovering now from her initial shock, was distraught. It wasn't Charlie's fault. He had only been doing what cats do. She just hadn't noticed him, and he hadn't made a sound. She didn't know how she was going to explain to Fergus that she had probably undone his weeks of patient encouragement with one false move.

She walked towards the gate, feeling more upset than she had bargained for. Glancing up the lane, in vain hope, she saw Charlie making his way slowly towards the fields.

Putting on her best 'Come kitty kitty' voice, she called to him. He turned towards her and sat down. She crouched low and continued to call. He stood up then sat down again, undecided. Lavinia found herself telling him she was sorry, it really was an accident. She promised him a tin of tuna if he came back.

That seemed to do the trick. Charlie got to his feet and slowly, slowly walked towards her, eyes fixed on her face. When he was close enough, she stood up and bent down to stroke his head. On impulse she picked him up and hugged him, but she put him down again fairly speedily. Hugs were not Charlie's thing.

Holding his tail high, he walked confidently ahead of her towards the back door, pausing once to check she was following as if to remind her that he hadn't had breakfast due to all the kerfuffle, and that she had promised him real tuna.

CHAPTER 17

Drama in W H Smith's

A momentary lapse in concentration was all it took to put Lavinia's body into free fall, propelling her, with speed and indignity, down the last few stairs in W H Smith's and dropping her in an untidy heap at the head of the Post Office queue.

'Wey hey lady!' someone yelled. 'That's a new way to get to the front.'

The ensuing chortle that rippled through the line was swiftly quelled by someone saying, 'Shut up you, she might be hurt.'

The door of the foreign currency kiosk flew open and a young woman emerged to take control. At least, from Lavinia's prone position, that appeared to be the general idea. Raising her head, she spied her glasses on the floor in front of her. Fearing someone might tread on them, she tried to free an arm from beneath her uncooperative body, only to find she couldn't move.

'My glasses,' she squeaked to the woman, who was now kneeling beside her.

'Don't worry love. I'll get them for you. That was quite a tumble. Have you got any pain anywhere?'

'No.'

'Can you wiggle your toes?'

'Yes, I feel okay but I'm not sure whether I can get up. I'm frightfully sorry to create a fuss. I really don't know what happened. I feel such an idiot.'

'It's easily done love. Missed your footing I expect. Old folks are doing it all the time on these stairs.'

If that was calculated to make Lavinia feel better, it failed. She did not take kindly to being lumped in a group of doddery old things with a propensity for hurling themselves into the Post Office.

In order to regain a modicum of control, she summoned up her willpower and succeeded in turning herself over. She was attempting to sit up when a stout woman, well 'spanxed' into a smart navy-blue suit, emerged from a door beside the kiosk. An oval badge on her lapel declared her to be a Supervisor.

'Assist the lady to sit up,' she barked at the woman

beside Lavinia. She continued as though ticking off items on an invisible list.

'Stand well back,' she instructed the small crowd, who were rapidly losing interest anyway.

'Ambulance call is in place, and can we have a chair over here?'

Miss Foreign Currency scuttled off to find one.

'Honestly, I think I'm fine. There's no need for an ambulance,' Lavinia protested as the two women helped her to stand. But she had to think again when a searing pain shot up her leg as her left foot came in to contact with the floor.

'Oh hell. I can't stand on that,' she shrieked and flopped onto the waiting chair with a shudder. She looked down at the hugely puffy ankle, protruding from her short, flat boot and her heart sank.

'Looks like an ambulance job to me,' said the navy-blue suit.

'Shall we have a look at that foot? Mmm, we can't blame this tumble on high heels, can we?' she said, tugging gingerly at the boot zip. Lavinia inhaled as the pain registered.

'I'm not in the habit of falling down stairs, in heels or otherwise,' she snapped, annoyed at the implication.

'Just a little joke madam,' said the suit, 'But judging by the swelling, I'm guessing you've done yourself a bit of mischief.'

The shock of being rendered horizontal without her consent was subsiding, but the pain at the end of her left leg had racked up a level and Lavinia's brain was racing. She was twelve miles from home, in the middle of the shopping centre. Her car was stranded in the multi-storey car park and she was about to be carted off to Accident and Emergency. She looked at her watch. One-thirty: Fergus would still be in his studio, anticipating her return and his lunch. He carried a mobile phone, reluctantly, but Fergus being Fergus, he only ever switched it on if *he* needed to contact *her*. She would have to wait until he was back in the house before ringing him.

She glanced across at the suit, who was now scribbling furiously on a clipboard.

Without looking up, the woman asked, 'Could I have your full name and home telephone number please? I need to file a report on what occurred.'

'I would have thought that was fairly obvious,' observed Lavinia. 'I fell down the stairs.'

'Quite so madam, regrettably so, but nevertheless, I am required to ascertain if there are any public liability issues, any malicious intent or whether the accident was caused purely by customer error.'

Lavinia raised her eyebrows.

'Are you familiar with these stairs madam? By which I mean, have you used them before?'

'Yes, of course. They are on a direct route to the car park, where, incidentally, my car is stuck and rapidly running out of time. What on earth can I do about that?'

'I can sort your car out with a phone call when I've done this. Don't worry, it can stay where it is until you can collect it – but if we could return to my report for a moment. Was anyone behind you or beside you on the stairs?'

'I suppose that's the official way of asking if I was pushed, clever. Difficult to say though. I was looking forwards as you'd expect. I don't recall any unusual jostling.'

'That's good,' said the suit. 'Now if I can have your details and those of the car, I'll go and make that phone call.'

Lavinia glanced at her watch. Fergus' hunger would have got the better of him by now. She took out her phone to call him and glared at yet another gawping child asking, 'Why is that old lady sitting there?' She curbed the urge to stick out her tongue.

Fergus' response echoed her own exasperation.

'Where the hell are you? I was expecting you back ages ago.'

'I'm still in town. I've...'

'You haven't crashed the car?'

'No, Fergus, the car is fine. However, I am not quite so fine.'

'I see. So when will you be back then?'

'Well, it's a little complicated because I have…'

'Just give me a rough idea. I've got eggs boiling and the timer thingy has just dinged.'

'Can you stop faffing about eggs for a moment Fergus and listen please? I've had a fall and hurt my ankle. I can't stand on it or drive, so I'm waiting for an ambulance to take me to A&E. The car is safe in the car park but I'll to need you to collect me later from the hospital.'

'Jeez! Lavinia, why didn't you say right away? Where exactly are you?'

'I'm in the Post Office in Smith's.'

'Okay, I'll get these eggs down me and then I'll be on my way.'

'Fergus, there is no rush. The ambulance hasn't arrived and there's bound to be a long wait in A&E.'

'No worries. It's hell's own job to find a parking space up there. Might take ages. Oh, incidentally, are you okay… the rest of you I mean, apart from the ankle?'

'Yes Fergus. I'm fine. I'll see you later.' As an afterthought she added, 'Can you switch on your phone?'

But Fergus had already hung up to attend to his eggs.

As she ended the call, a bearded young man in a hi-vis jacket bounded down the stairs. He flung down an enormous backpack and sat on the steps in front of her.

'Hi, I'm Chris. Paramedic. Apologies for the delay. Your name is?'

'Lavinia Moreton.'

'Lavinia, lovely name. Well, Lavinia, unfortunately your ambulance was diverted to a smash on the motorway. It's a bit of a mad afternoon I'm afraid.'

Lavinia attempted a smile.

He continued, 'I'm usually in the office, but I've been drafted out into the field, so to speak, to ease the pressure. I believe you've had a fall. Is that correct?'

Before Lavinia could reply, the suit reappeared.

'Have you brought a wheelchair? The lady's ankle is damaged, and she can't stand on it. So, unless you are expecting her to hop up the stairs to street level or are planning a fireman's lift, you are going to need wheels to get her out of here.'

'Ah,' said Chris, tugging his beard. 'That could be a problem.' He turned to Lavinia, 'Can I have a quick look at the ankle?'

He lifted her foot and rested it on his knee in a bizarre Prince Charming moment. He shook his head.

'Not very pretty is it? Can you move your foot left and right?'

Lavinia made a feeble attempt and winced.

'Try up and down.'

Lavinia screwed her eyes tight as the pain intensified. He put her foot down gently.

'I'll get on to control from the car and see what the ambulance situation is. Sorry about this. I won't be a tick.'

The suit offered Lavinia a bottle of water, 'on the house', but acutely aware that it could be some time before she could get to a loo, Lavinia limited herself to tiny sips. She tried Fergus again, but he'd gone incommunicado.

Chris flopped down again on to the steps, grinning.

'They're sending an ambulance from outside the area, so we've got plenty of time to get to know each other.'

He laughed at Lavinia's expression as he rummaged in the backpack.

'Don't worry, it won't be too long. We'll do some paperwork and some obs to keep ourselves amused. Pop this on your finger for starters.'

He connected her up to a black box from the bag.

'Now, if you can slip the other arm out of your coat, I'll check your blood pressure. Any shortness of breath or pain other than in the foot?'

Lavinia shook her head, trying to block out the scrutiny of people going up and down the stairs.

'Might as well do an ECG while you've got your coat off,' said Chris, hauling out another machine.

'Not in here, surely!' wailed Lavinia.

'Fret not dear lady. No exposed flesh, I promise.'

It was four o'clock by the time he'd completed a battery of tests, sorted out his 'paperwork', which was a series of clicks and swipes on his iPad, and regaled her with his plans for the weekend. Fergus would probably have been waiting for about two hours at the hospital. Lavinia figured his tolerance meter would have already blown a gasket, but his phone was still off. She sighed. There was absolutely nothing she could do to change anything.

The other paramedics, when they finally arrived, were a double act. Dave, all of five foot five inches, carried a portable wheelchair in one hand and a huge bag slung over the opposite shoulder. His partner, Mick, six foot plus, carried a pale blue blanket draped over one arm. Having introduced themselves to Lavinia and listened to Chris' summing up, they set about immobilising Lavinia's leg in an orange air bag before transferring her expertly into the wheelchair, now draped with the blanket.

'Comfortable m'lady?' enquired Mick, plonking Lavinia's bag on her lap and proceeding to swaddle her and her bag with half the blanket.

'I really don't need wrapping up,' she said crossly, extricating her hands. 'I've got a coat on.'

'Ah,' said Mick, taking her hands and enclosing them beneath the other side of the blanket before tucking it firmly down the side of the seat.

'You see Madam, it's not about keeping you warm, it's about keeping you safe between here and the vehicle.'

'We're in a shopping centre for heaven's sake, not a war zone,' retorted Lavinia.

Mick chuckled. 'Explain to the lady about the blanket Dave, while I put the gear back in the bag.'

Little Dave leaned over her shoulder from behind the wheelchair. 'Health and Safety regulations regarding persons and possessions in transit, madam. Wouldn't want some little toe-rag hiking off with your handbag while you've only got one good leg, would we? Or you trapping your hand in a door perhaps. Especially not when I'm driving the chair.'

'Well, I hope you've got a bag to put over my head too in case anyone recognises me.'

Chris fastened up his backpack. 'Best give in Lavinia. You don't have a leg to stand on with these two. Just sit back and enjoy the ride.' He wished her well, high-fived Dave and bounded away.

With forensic clarity Lavinia suddenly saw herself as the three young men saw her; a crotchety old dear who had got herself into a fix and needed to be rescued. It was a sobering picture which carried scores of others in its wake. She submitted to the chair and the blanket. Her ankle was throbbing.

'Ready to roll then Dave?' Mick asked as he slung the bag over his shoulder. 'We're going to take the scenic route back to the vehicle Lavinia. No lift in this area apparently. So, are you comfortable?'

'Yes, thank you,' she murmured.

It was cold in the gloomy passages of the shopping centre's underbelly. A network of piping and vast bundles of cables lined the walls. Mick and Dave squabbled amiably, their voices echoing in the deserted tunnel. A goods lift took them up to street level and Lavinia blinked at the bright lights of Next in front of her. She cast her eyes down as Dave navigated the wheelchair through bustling shoppers to the waiting ambulance.

Once she was safely inside, Mick strapped her onto a stretcher, attached her to a heart and blood pressure monitor and then sat beside her while Dave negotiated the early evening traffic.

'Can you go home after this trip?' Lavinia asked.

'No chance. Cuppa tea might be nice though. We came on at ten this morning and haven't had a lunch break yet. It's a crazy day today.'

'I expect you could do without silly old women falling down stairs then.'

'All in a day's work my dear. Accidents happen. Be out of a job if they didn't. Sorry about your long wait though. You got someone to meet you at the hospital?'

'Yes, my husband.'

She hadn't given Fergus a thought for some time. Checking her watch, she saw it was five-fifteen. Her heart sank. Fergus would be at the end of his piece of string.

Lavinia spotted him as soon as Dave wheeled her into the waiting area. He was sitting, elbows on his knees, chin on his hands, staring disconsolately at his shoes. Lavinia sensed the tension around him. He started when her padded orange leg appeared close to his nose and stood up, flustered.

'Are you the registered owner of this lovely lady, sir?' asked Dave.

'Well, that's, er, certainly one way of putting it, yes,' burbled Fergus with a wild grin.

'Right then sir, she's all yours. I hope you've got your pinny primed for action. I don't think she'll be doing any Hoovering for a little while.' He laughed and patted Lavinia's shoulder. 'You make sure he takes good care of you now.'

Lavinia smiled weakly at that prospect and thanked him. She watched him saunter in the direction of the cafeteria, almost sad to see him go. She had felt safe with Dave and Mick.

CHAPTER 18

Festive Spirit

Lavinia took the coffee tray into the conservatory and turned on the heater. It was chilly despite the winter sunshine. Fergus was already outside, pruning roses to make space for a ladder and two men who were coming to fix a leak in the roof. Lavinia tapped the window and held up the coffee pot. Fergus gave her a thumbs up and continued his indiscriminate snipping. She winced in sympathy with her roses, but they were established bushes, so they'd probably forgive him come the spring.

Wrapping her hands around her mug, Lavinia surveyed the garden. It was tidy and neat for the winter. 'Manageable' was how Fergus put it. Lavinia's deep herbaceous borders, fragrant rose arches, soft fruit, and the poly-tunnel where she'd grown melons and aubergines, had all been relegated to photograph albums, history along with the lawn tractor. Aching backs and creaking knees had persuaded Lavinia and Fergus to modify the garden so that it was less time consuming and more… manageable. Of course, the carpets of snowdrops would still emerge in early spring, followed by daffodils and the delicate pinks and purples of Joseph and Mary.

Lavinia put her mug down and rubbed her hands together. She twiddled her wedding ring. Conscious of her knobbly knuckles, she checked that she could still get it off; only just.

With a sigh she refilled her mug and banged on the window at Fergus. He mouthed an 'okaay' at her and disappeared in the direction of the shed, with the green bin in tow. Lavinia frowned when moments later he came into the conservatory, drying his hands on his trousers.

'There's a towel for your hands you know. I'm afraid the coffee isn't very hot. You've been out there ages.'

'Don't fret. It'll be fine.'

She watched him flop into a chair, slopping coffee on the tiled floor, and resisted the urge to mop it up immediately. They sat quietly for several minutes before Fergus spoke.

'Sometimes I feel bloody useless these days. I did all the jobs round here you know. Hedges, trees, painting, everything. I could have done the roof too. Just seem to have lost my oomph lately.'

'Fergus, you're seventy-six. No-one expects you to be shinning up ladders any more and there is no shame in paying a man to do it.'

'Yes, I know that, but it's a bit of a bugger, this old age stuff. I do hope the roof guy makes a good job of it.'

'Of course he will. Stop mithering. We'll be all sorted by Christmas. You'll see.'

'Oh heck! You aren't starting that palaver already? Can't we bypass the madness for once, just chuck out the calendar and put up a new one?'

'Fergus, you really are a miserable old curmudgeon at this time of year. Well, all year actually, but particularly in December. Where's your festive spirit, for heaven's sake?'

'Never had one old thing. Thought you'd have worked that one out.' He drained his coffee, stood up and stretched his back.

'Wouldn't mind some of those spicy Christmas cookies from Aldi though if you happen to be going in that direction.'

He ducked automatically. But Lavinia didn't have anything at hand to hurl at him, so he slunk off towards the stairs.

'I'm going to talk to the drum,' he called.

Lavinia pulled out her Christmas card list from the back

of her address book and took a pen from the pot on the windowsill. There were more names to cross out this year. Fergus had lost a couple of family members and two of her close friends had succumbed to chronic ailments. She decided to write a new list and sidestep the stark confrontation with human frailty.

Lavinia had always loved Christmas. She had spent a lifetime trying to generate some enthusiasm in Fergus and was still trying. But he had no interest in festive trappings. He considered cards a waste of money and paper, and his approach to Yuletide fare ranged from indifference through to antagonism. Egg and chips remained his favourite meal, preferably followed by trifle or ice cream. Just once in their life together, Lavinia had indulged Fergus in this respect. They'd thrown tradition to the ducks and high tailed off to the coast on Christmas Day, only to discover that hordes of others had had the same idea. After a bracing walk along the beach, avoiding the novice kite flyers, and small children who'd been determined to ask Santa for a bucket and spade, they'd quaffed soup from a thermos and headed home to the chip pan.

Early in their relationship, Fergus had discovered that Lavinia's need for a Christmas tree was non-negotiable and ever since, he had adhered to her rules about shiny paper and labels before placing his present for her beneath the tree and beside her gift for him. Every year Lavinia bought Fergus a few extra inexpensive gifts, drawing pencils, socks, or chocolate truffles, a gesture he had always found vaguely embarrassing.

'You don't need to do all this you know,' he'd say.

'I know I don't. But it's what I've always done at Christmas, so, for better or for worse and all that. You signed up same as me. Remember?'

'Mmm' he said, 'I suppose.'

Towards the middle of December, Fergus began to psych himself up for the shopping marathon. At this time of year Lavinia seemed possessed by a pathological need to cover all eventualities, from unexpected vegetarians to earthquakes and everything in between. In vain, Fergus protested. 'It's only two days, for God's sake!'

'Actually, it's ten if you need anything other than toilet rolls or tinned rice pudding and it's winter. Anything could happen.'

'So when was the last disastrous thing then?'

'You're being obstructive, Fergus. The longer it was, the more likely it becomes.'

He could have argued the point, but thought better of it. 'But you are permanently prepared for the apocalypse old thing. Er... have we got any tinned rice pudding, by the way?'

'Fergus, if you don't want to help just say so. It's not a problem. I can go on my own.'

'Don't be daft, you can't manage heavy bags by yourself. I'll get the car out. Let's just go and do it, now.'

'I'll be a couple of minutes,' she shouted as he struggled into his anorak and disappeared outside.

She sorted out bags and lists, found the scarf that matched her coat, changed her shoes, and switched off lights. She was about to lock up when Charlie appeared for his second breakfast. She was setting down a dish of cat munchies outside as Fergus thundered round the corner of the house.

'Never mind the cat. He won't die of starvation. We could be halfway there in the time it takes to get you out of the house.'

Lavinia glared, pocketed the key and hurried to the car, just as it started to rain.

'I don't see why it has to be a rush all of a sudden. And you might at least wait while I fasten my seat belt.'

The car, already halfway down the lane, was beeping frantically, as usual, about a loose occupant. The windscreen wipers flicked back and forth with an irritating squeak as Fergus drove on in silence. After several minutes Lavinia observed, 'We need new wiper blades'.

'They'll be okay for a bit yet. I'll put a squirt of washing-up stuff in the screen wash.'

'I'd have thought it was worth getting them done, considering that the winter is looming. We *could* just pop into Halfords. They do it for you in no time.'

'Lavinia, there is enough to do today without faffing about wiper blades. Just put the radio on and stop fretting.'

She didn't reply, but it struck her that Fergus was becoming ever more adept at finding ways to avoid things he didn't want to do.

Fergus was drumming in his head. Jonny McFadden had released a new YouTube video. It was a tricky rhythm and Fergus had planned to spend the morning working on it to expand his repertoire. It was in his interests to get the shopathon ticked off.

As soon as he'd parked the car, he despatched Lavinia to collect a trolley while he reorganised the boot space. And in so doing he created a hiatus which allowed life another opportunity to play tricks.

In charge of the trolley for once, Lavinia veered off into Flowers and lingered over her choice of carnations or chrysanthemums before she engaged with Vegetables. Fergus, with eyes skinned, plunged straight into the melee but couldn't spot Lavinia among the women who were fervently foraging for the best broccoli heads. The realisation that he didn't have the faintest idea what she was wearing unsettled him, and as he bumbled through the shoppers looking for clues, a crazy scenario played in his head. It involved a police officer questioning him about Lavinia's disappearance.

'Can you describe your wife for me sir?'

'Erm, grey hair ... and glasses.'

'Bit vague sir. What was she wearing the last time you saw her?'

'Buggered if I know officer.'

'Jeez,' thought Fergus as he wandered deeper into the store. 'Where the hell has she got to?'

Lavinia finally caught up with him in Dairy and Ready to Eat. He was standing with his back to the olives, hands thrust deep into his pockets. Without the trolley to hang on to, he looked strangely incomplete.

'Where the hell did you go?' he hissed.

'Nowhere. I picked up some flowers and then did the veg. I thought you were still outside chatting to someone.'

'I came straight in after you, but I couldn't see you and I wasn't sure what you were wearing. I guessed it was probably your green jacket, so I followed that woman over there by the cheese. I wasn't too sure about the bobble hat but everything else looked about right. I almost chucked some Double Gloucester in her trolley and wheeled it off. I don't know if you are aware of this, but you do it to me all the time in shops. You wander off in pursuit of something and then I can't find you.'

'Oh, for goodness' sake Fergus! You sound like a toddler. I'm sorry if I do that. But it might help if you were actually in your body when we're out instead of doing a set with Jonny McFadden in your head.'

'Okay, okay. But just look at her, Lavinia. It was an easy mistake to make.'

The woman, who was now in Yoghurts, was indeed similar in height and build to Lavinia. She was wearing navy trousers, black shoes, and the exact same green jacket. Her grey hair, glasses and black canvas shoulder bag, confirmed Lavinia's mirror image – except for the bobble hat. Bobble hats had never featured among Lavinia's favoured accessories. She grinned at Fergus.

'I'm going to tell her,' she said. And before he could stop her she had tapped the woman on the shoulder, and the two of them were in fits of laughter.

Fergus bent over the trolley and pushed on in search of his favourite beer. In his limited experience, a woman usually ran a mile from another in the same outfit and he couldn't quite work out what had happened back there, or why it had left him feeling a little disconcerted.

A promotional display of Apple Brandy barged in on his musings at that moment and his eyes homed in on the word 'Calvados'. Instantly, pictures of Normandy orchards surfaced in his mind. He could almost taste the fragrant liqueur, feel the tingle on his tongue and the comforting warmth as it caressed his throat. He thought about the old lady who had given him a sugar lump with his first glass when he was a young man. She'd winked at him and told him it was 'the French way'. As he recalled the afterglow that followed several more shots, his hand reached out for a bottle of the amber liquid without even registering the price.

'What the hell,' he thought. 'She said I needed some festive spirit. This is just the ticket.' He took care to place the bottle in amongst his beers to deflect Lavinia's eagle eye and moved swiftly on into Rice and Pasta before she caught up with him.

When the shopping, to cover all eventualities, was paid for, packed and loaded into the boot, Fergus was dismayed to learn that the mission still had a way to go. The bird had to be ordered from the butcher. Stamps were required from the Post Office, where there was a queue spilling out into the street, and Lavinia's list for the pharmacy made him weak at the knees.

'I understand the need for Paracetamol, Strepsils and Rennies, but why do we need peppermint oil capsules, eye drops and Sudafed?'

'Because the ones I've got are out of date.'

'Have we ever needed them?'

'No, but we might.'

Weighed down with bags of bird seed and peanuts, Fergus was still chuntering as he trudged along behind Lavinia.

'I really don't understand why women don't stand

sideways while they natter on pavements. They are all over the place, blocking the way with their bloody shopping trolleys. What with women, dogs and screaming kids, it's madness out here. And don't even think about venturing into that market over there. Whatever they've got we can live without it.'

'Oh, cheer up Fergus. Can't you dredge up a smidgen of goodwill to all women for once?'

'Not for this lot, no, I can't. Are you nearly finished now? I'm just about done in. Can we go home?'

'The only thing I haven't got is...'

'Oh, would you look at that!' Fergus interrupted. 'They've got daffodils over there. That's what we need. Here, you look after this stuff. I'll just nip across and get some.'

Handing Lavinia all the bags, he promptly shot across the road and disappeared into the teeming market, leaving her open-mouthed and blocking the pavement. Several minutes passed before he emerged, grinning like a small boy with a bag of toffees. He was clutching several bunches of daffodil buds.

'What luck eh? They might come out for Christmas Day if we keep them cool and then bring them indoors. What do you think, old thing? Aren't these just the best thing to lift your spirits and cheer you up?'

Lavinia summoned a weak smile. All these years and nothing had changed. They were still chalk and cheese.